To Lisa

God gives joy!

Show Someone Love!

Love Notes

100 DAYS OF SEEKING AND AFFIRMING GOD'S LOVE

F. Bruce Williams

DR. F. BRUCE WILLIAMS

First Printing: 2015

ISBN: **1511980915**
ISBN-13:**978-1511980913**

fbw@fbrucewilliamsministries.com

www.fbrucewilliamsministries.com

DEDICATION

This book is dedicated to those who affirm God's love

and seek to share God's love with others.

ACKNOWLEDGEMENTS

First, I thank and praise the Lord for the opportunity to serve. It is my prayer that this small offering will bless others and glorify God.

Thanks to the disciples of Bates Memorial Church for being a constant source of inspiration and for providing me the opportunity to write. I love you all!

A huge "Thank You" to Hannah Drake, my extraordinary Administrative Assistant. The 100 Days 100 Acts of Love Campaign at Bates that inspired me to write these daily devotionals was her brain child! Thanks for assisting me in editing my work and for choosing the book cover. Hannah, words cannot express my appreciation for you and your selfless support.

Helen Johnson, thank you so very much for editing the manuscript. Thanks for not only doing meticulous work, but also for your generous spirit.

To the staff of Bates, thank you for giving me space to create. Your faithfulness means I can write without anxiety.

Finally, a very special thanks to my wonderful wife, best friend and lover, Michelle. The truth is I would never be able to accomplish anything of substance without her endless support, unconditional love and constant faith in me. Michelle, you are my world. I adore you.

INTRODUCTION

2015 marked the Centennial for Bates Memorial Church, a fellowship of Christian disciples in Louisville, Kentucky, whom I have had the privilege of Pastoring for almost 30 years. We started 2015 with great excitement and were curious about how we were going to celebrate being a part of a 100 year legacy of Christian service. In one of my many brainstorming sessions with my Administrative Assistant, Hannah Drake, she suggested that we celebrate our Centennial by encouraging our congregation to show acts of love. Since it was our Centennial she recommended that we set aside 100 days. From this was born the 100 Days 100 Acts of Love campaign where we would encourage the congregation at Bates Memorial to show at least one act of love to someone each day for the first 100 days of the year. We even provided as a promotional tool, red rubber wrist bands with the campaign slogan on it for all of the participants to wear, another excellent idea from Hannah. We were confident that this would be a blessing for the congregation and community. We planned for the campaign to connect to our annual church anniversary and what was so exciting about that decision was that from January 1 up to the weekend that we usually celebrate our annual church anniversary was 100 days! Talking about divine confirmation! As a source of inspiration, I decided to provide a written devotional message that could be read at the start of each day of the 100 Days 100 Acts of Love campaign called Love Notes, hence the title of this book. Each love note was not only designed to bless the reader, but also to encourage the reader to show some act of love to someone during that day. You will notice that at the end of each devotional is the admonition "show someone some love." I hope these devotionals will serve as an inspiration to you as well. You might want to use this book to start your own campaign of love through your own church or organization or you can simply use it to assist you in your own personal daily devotional time. However you choose to use it, my prayer is that Love Notes will connect you with the love of God and inspire you to share that love with others.

Love Note 1

"... your strength will equal your days (New International Version, Deut. 33.25b)."

This love note is a precious promise from God that we can claim. This promise initially came in the form of a prophetic promise from Moses to the Tribe of Asher. Moses could declare these words because he had witnessed in his own life how God had given him strength equal to his days. There is strength for the quantity of your days. No matter how long you live, God will give you sufficient strength. There is strength for the quality of your days. Whatever kind of day you have, God will grant sufficient strength. The harder the day, the greater the strength. This promise flows from the

9

loving heart of our great God. Claim this promise and with a heart of gratitude, use your strength to show someone some love!

~ ~ ~ ~ ~

Prayer

Dear Lord, thank you for being the strength that I need for the challenges of every day. Be my strength this day so that I might do what pleases you. I claim the promise of your strength and walk in that strength today and every day. In Jesus name, Amen.

Love Note 2

"The eternal God is your refuge, and underneath are the everlasting arms (Deut. 33.27a)."

Whatever today brings, remember this love note. First, God is our refuge. God is the place where we can hide, a place of safety and security when the stormy blasts of life are too much for us. Second, God is our eternal support. God holds us up with God's arms, like a parent holds a child. God's arms are loving, strong, capable and secure. In fact, they are everlasting arms, reliable arms. What a wonderful God we serve! Finally, realize that in order for God to care for us in such an intimate way means that God is close. So whenever it gets dark, remember that the darkness is never evidence of His absence, but it is the shadow of God's arm as He pulls us close to His chest. Knowing you have such love, go out today and show someone some love!

~ ~ ~ ~ ~

Prayer

Strong God, I am grateful that you are my place of safety and security. Help me to never forget that you are forever with me, close and caring. Today, I give glory in care of your strong and capable arms and I walk through the day knowing that there is safety in you. In the name of Christ I pray, Amen.

Love Note 3

"Give thanks to The Lord, for he is good; his love endures forever (Ps. 118.1, 29)."

This verse appears at both the beginning and the end of the Psalm. I suppose the truth of the verse was such a blessing that the writer had to say it twice! We have a reason to give thanks to God. Why? God is good! It may be trite, but it is true: "God is good all the time, and all the time God is good!" The goodness of God is a statement about the character of God. The essence of God is that God is good. Since God is good by nature, then all that God does is automatically good! God is also a God of love. God loves you and there is nothing you can do to make God love you any more or any less.

God loves you totally, completely, absolutely, unconditionally! The love that God has for us has no expiration date! God will never stop loving us! In light of that kind of love, if you haven't already, you ought to give your life to God through Jesus Christ! Having received that love, go out and show someone some love!

~ ~ ~ ~ ~

Prayer

Loving God, I rejoice today in your goodness and your love. I am especially glad that your goodness and love are forever directed toward me. Today, my heart is filled with praise and thanksgiving and I will not be ashamed to share the joy. Thank you for being so good and kind to me. I pray this in the sweetest name I know, Jesus Christ, Amen.

Love Note 4

"And we know that in all things God works for the good of those who love him, who have been called according to his purpose (Ro. 8.28)."

This is one of the most familiar and popular verses in the Bible, and for good reason. This verse testifies that God has the incredible ability to work everything for the good of those who belong to Him. All things that happen to us may not be good, but God is so incredible that God can get in the middle of all things and bring good out of them. Even when the most negative and horrendous things happy in life, God can work for your good. The greatest Biblical example of this is the crucifixion and resurrection of Jesus. The cross and the subsequent empty tomb are evidence that God can bring life out of death. If what we are dealing with in life is not worse than death, then what are we worried about? If God can bring life out of death, humanity's greatest enemy, then God can and is working all things out for our good. Hallelujah! Since God loves you like that, today, go out and show someone some love.

~ ~ ~ ~ ~

Prayer

Dear God, I stand amazed at the fact that you are in all things in my life, working out all things for my good. I am in awe of you and how you can take even the bad things and use them to fulfil your destiny in my life. So today, I thank you for all things, even the bad, because I know you can and will use them for my good. No matter what happens today, I know that you will use it for my good. I Christ's name I pray, Amen.

Love Note 5

"Cast all your anxiety on him because he cares for you (1 Pe.5.7)."

Life can be full of worry and anxiety at times. We are tempted to fret and complain about the cares of this life. We often carry cares in our hearts and emotions like heavy weights that serve no other purpose but to discourage us and tempt us to complain, quit and even begin to wonder if God really cares. The scriptures teach that we never have to wonder if God cares. God does care for us. No matter who we are and what we are going through, God cares. Since God is God, God is able to handle what we are not able to handle. God is able to carry what turns out to be too much for us to carry. God is a strong, caring God who invites us not to carry life's cares alone. When the cares of life are too much, we can throw or cast our cares on God. Give your cares to God by faith, believing that God can and will work them out. God takes our cares because God loves us. So, go out and show someone some love.

~ ~ ~ ~ ~

Prayer

Caring God, today I refuse to carry the burdens of life on my own. I choose to cast them all on you. I promise, each moment of the day, to do my best to place them all in your capable hands by trusting them all to you, knowing that you truly care about me. In the strong name of Jesus I pray, Amen.

Love Note 6

"Your word is a lamp for my feet, a light on my path (Ps.119.105)."

One of the things I appreciate about God is that God has preserved the Bible through the centuries so that we might use it for wise and divine guidance to help us live our lives. David makes a profound statement about the value of the word in his life. God's Word serves as a lamp or light to guide us through the twists and turns of life. Knowing the Word of God and applying it to our life is like having a light that lights dark paths so that we will know which way to go. Physical light helps to guide our steps and our stops! The light of God's Word does the same. It is exciting to know that in a world full of uncertainties that we have the Word to help us navigate through life! The Word of God can guide us in our decisions regarding family, finances, relationships, careers, and can even help us discern right from wrong. We can really appreciate God's Word best when it is time to make decisions about the things in life that mean the most. God must really love us to provide such a precious resource. Now, go out and show someone some love.

~ ~ ~ ~ ~

Prayer

Gracious God, I rejoice that you have left your Word to guide me through life's journey. Today, I claim afresh the worth of your Word and recommit myself to letting your Word be my guide. I confess today that I live by no greater word than your Word. Thank you for this precious resource. In the name of the Word made flesh I pray, Amen.

Love Note 7

"Have I not commanded you? Be strong and courageous. Do not be afraid; do not be discouraged, for the Lord your God will be with you wherever you go (Jos. 1.9)."

Can you hear these words echoing through the corridors of history finding a meaningful place in your heart even now? No matter what the day brings, no matter what you have to face, let these words encourage you to be strong and courageous. Maybe there is an intimidating trial or difficult test you have to face today. Whatever it is, be strong and face it with courage. Why? Because God promises that he will be with you wherever you go; and if God be with you, God is more than anything that is against you. So, take courage today! Be strong today! Go in the certainty that God goes before you. By faith, walk in the promise of the presence of God knowing that regardless of what you have to face, God is more than enough! Now walk in that assurance and show someone some love.

~ ~ ~ ~ ~

Prayer

Precious Lord, sometimes life is difficult and intimidating, but today I hear your voice telling me to be strong and courageous. By faith I will walk in that call knowing that I am not alone; and, since you are with me, I am not afraid. In Jesus name I pray, Amen.

Love Note 8

"I thank my God every time I remember you (Php.1.3)."

Is there a person or persons in your life who, whenever you think of them, the memory of them warms your heart? This is how the Apostle Paul felt towards the believers in the city of Philippi. One of the most precious gifts that God has given to us are friends whose love brings us great joy and gratitude. Paul had been so loved by the Philippian fellowship that whenever he thought of them, he was not only filled with joy, he was also moved to thank God for them! I am certain there is no greater gift than the gift of true friends. Even when you are not physically with them, the very memory of their love can strengthen you and inspire your heart. Do you have a friend like that? If you don't, why not be that kind of friend? Go out and show someone some love.

~~~~~

Prayer

Father, today I am reminded of the precious gift of friendship. Forgive me for taking good friends for granted. Thank you for the joy and support that my friends bring into my life. Teach me how to be a better friend to others and most of all, thank you for being my best Friend. In the Name of Jesus Christ I pray, Amen.

Love Note 9

"Let us not become weary in doing good, for at the proper time we will reap a harvest if we do not give up (Gal. 6.9)."

Few Christians like to admit it, but sometimes we get tired of doing good. Sometimes we become tired of doing "good," because at times, our efforts seem fruitless and vain. Few things can discourage us like working hard and long, but seeing little or no results. It becomes especially difficult when it seems that others who are doing "good" are getting results, but no matter how much "good" we do, we seem to get no results at all. Well, there are two reasons we should keep doing "good' anyway. First, because we are commanded to. Besides, it's always "good" to do "good." Secondly, because doing "good" is never ultimately in vain. The scriptures maintain that the reason we have not seen any results is that it's just not our season yet. But seasons change. Your season is coming. If you can stay faithful, when your season finally comes, "you will reap...if you do not give up." Now, go do "good" by showing someone some love.

~ ~ ~ ~ ~

Prayer

Dear Lord, I confess that there are times when I am just tired of doing "good." The work of the Kingdom can be tedious and sometimes seems in vain. Forgive me when I've doubted the worth of your work. Today I claim the promise that perseverance brings fruitfulness. I will work today knowing that my season will come. And when it does, I will give you praise for the harvest. In the meantime, I will be faithful and I will give you praise in advance. In the name of the Christ I pray, Amen.

Love Note 10

"...give thanks in all circumstances; for this is God's will for you in Christ Jesus (1 Th. 5.18)."

God seeks to cultivate within each of us an attitude of gratitude; so, the scriptures declare that we are to give thanks in all circumstances. Notice, it does not say give thanks for all circumstances. The idea is that we learn how to be thankful in the midst of any circumstance. There may be circumstances where we give thanks "because of" the circumstances. There may be circumstances where we give thanks "in spite of" the circumstances. Either way, the will of God is that we learn to give thanks in the midst of any circumstance. Thanksgiving is to be an abiding attitude of the heart in the face of shifting circumstances. This attitude gives power and buoyancy to the inner spirit. It can also open our eyes to things or people we sometimes take for granted. The truth is, we have a lot to be thankful for. Besides, there is one reason we can always be thankful – God loves us no matter what! Nothing can change that. Now, go show someone some love.

~~~~~

Prayer

Dear Lord, I realize that I have so much to be grateful for. Thank you for reminding me that gratitude is always in order. No matter what the situation today, I will be encouraged by the fact that in the midst of all of life's circumstances, I have so many reasons to be grateful: the greatest reason being that you love me no matter what! In the loving name of Jesus I pray, Amen.

Love Note 11

"And let us consider how we may spur one another on toward love and good deeds, not give up meeting together, as some are in the habit of doing, but encouraging one another-and all the more as you see the Day approaching (Heb. 10.24-25)."

If God is our, Father then we must have a family. One special family we have is the church. God has provided us a spiritual family so that we can have a place to belong. Even the strongest believer needs somewhere to belong. The scriptures encourage us to make sure that we maintain the habit of gathering together as the family of God for worship and fellowship. One of the benefits of gathering together is that the fellowship serves as a place where we can encourage one another to live a life of love and service. Life can be a struggle at times and we can be tempted to revert to living a selfish, self-centered life. However, the fellowship of the people of God can serve to remind us that we are called to live like our Savior whose life was the epitome of love and service. Love inspired Him to serve humanity by giving His life that we might have eternal life. As His disciples, we are called to love and serve others. Believe it or not, that kind of life brings fulfillment and joy! So, go out now and show someone some love.

~~~~~

Prayer

Heavenly Father, forgive me for failing to appreciate the gift of the church that you have given to every believer and to the world. Thank you for the love, support, instruction and encouragement that I gain from the church. I commit to do my part to be present, available and a source of encouragement for my

church family. I also commit to be the church in the world and live a life of service like my Savior. In Jesus name I pray, Amen.

Love Note 12

"The king will reply, 'Truly I tell you, whatever you did for one of the least of these brothers and sisters of mine, you did for me (Matt. 25.40)."

God loves everyone no matter who they are. However, the Bible seems to indicate that God is especially attentive and concerned about "the least of these." It makes sense, when you think about it, because those are the ones in society who are the most vulnerable and are often without an advocate. God is especially attentive to them and desires that we be especially attentive to them as well. In fact, the Bible reads in such a way that it gives the impression that God takes how we treat the most vulnerable among us personally. Jesus declared,

"When you did it to the least of these...you did it to me." That means that we have a wonderful opportunity to behave toward the most vulnerable with the kindness, compassion and care that they need and God desires. Imagine the joy we can bring to the lives of "the least of these" through our sincere acts of love. It will fill the heart of the Father with joy! Go now and show someone some love.

~~~~~

Prayer

Compassionate King, I adore you for your love of humanity, especially for those who are the most vulnerable. I covet your heart of care. So fill my heart afresh with your Spirit of compassion today. Teach me kindness and courage so that I can be your love in the world, especially for the weak. Thank you for the chance to fill your heart with joy by serving you through the least of these. In Jesus name, the serving Savior, I pray, Amen.

Love Note 13

"Praise be to the God and Father of our Lord Jesus Christ, the Father of compassion and the God of all comfort, who comforts us in all our troubles....(1 Co.1.3-4a)."

The Apostle Paul characterizes God as "the Father... who comforts us in all our troubles." Life is full of troubles. There is just no way around it. All of us have our share of troubles, all types of troubles. There are all kind of ways that we seek to bring comfort to ourselves in times of trouble. Some ways are constructive and, unfortunately, some ways are destructive. It's good to know that in those times when we need comfort, God is available to comfort us. God can comfort because God is "the God of all comfort." God may comfort us by changing our situation or God may choose to comfort us in the midst of our uncomfortable situation. God may use the word, communion with Him in prayer, or even a special person to comfort you. Take comfort in knowing that in times of trouble, if we would turn to God and seek God's presence, God will show that He is a divine parent who comforts. Receive, by faith, God's comfort today. Now, face the day, showing someone some love.

~~~~~

Prayer

God of all comfort, there are times when this world can be so hard and harsh. I praise you for the comfort that only you can give. Thank for you for caring enough to come to my rescue and give me the comfort I need to heal and grow. As I move through the day, I will be mindful that no matter what may happen, you are available to bring me comfort in my time of need. In Jesus name I pray, Amen.

Love Note 14

"...so that we can comfort those in any trouble with the comfort we ourselves have received from God (1 Co. 1.4b)."

According to the scriptures, God is a God of comfort who can bring comfort to those of us who need it. Any trouble we have to face, God is a comforter. Any hardship we have to face, God is a comforter. Today's scripture reveals to us that the comfort provided to us by God in times of trouble is not for our benefit alone! When God comforts us, it gives us the opportunity to comfort others with the comfort "we ourselves have received from God." God gives comfort to us so that God can get comfort through us to others who may need comforting! Those who are recipients of comfort are now called and qualified to be a source of comfort for others. Through God's comfort, our pain is transformed into the power to help comfort others in their times of pain. The healed can become healers. The helped can become helpers. The blessed can become a blessing! Take that truth with you today and show someone some love!

~~~~~

Prayer

Dear Lord, I enter this day grateful that you are the God of all comfort. I am especially thankful that you can use me to be a conduit of comfort for those in need. Show me how to draw from the comfort I have found in you to bring comfort to the hurting that may cross my path today. In Jesus name I pray, Amen.

Love Note 15

"You are the light of the world...let your light shine before men, that they may see your good deeds and praise your Father in heaven (Matt. 5.14a,16)."

Jesus declares that we who are his disciples are "the light of the world." The implications of this truth is that we live in a dark world. As representatives of Jesus and the Kingdom of God, we are to shine. One way we shine is by the good deeds we do. The Bible teaches that Jesus went about doing good. We are to go about doing the same. We are not saved by good works, but we are saved to do good works. When we go about doing good in a world that is so often void of good, not only will people in need be blessed, but others will take notice. When they do, because we represent our Savior, God will get the glory. People will see our deeds and because of who we are, will praise our God! The good we do comes from the God in us. So God gets the credit and the praise. Perhaps as our deeds direct people to God, maybe they too will become followers of Christ and join us in filling the world with good deeds rooted in a good God! Let's go out today and through good deeds, show someone some love.

~~~~~

Prayer

God of light and love, thank you for choosing me to reflect the light of your love in the world. The light that shines in me is not my light, it is yours. I am but a candle that bears your light. Teach me to use your light as a light to guide others and not as a floodlight to blind others. Let every act of love I show today somehow point others to you, revealing that you are indeed a God of love. In the name of Jesus, the greatest

light, I pray, Amen.

Love Note 16

"...remembering the words the Lord himself said: 'It is more blessed to give than to receive (Ac. 20.35)."

Here the Apostle Paul quotes our Lord. What is striking about these words is that they are the exact opposite of what the world teaches. Our country and culture teach that the best and most blessed thing is to receive. That's our culture's greatest joy and deepest desire – to receive. What Jesus teaches turns it upside down (or right side up if you receive this as Truth). One is blessed when one receives. All of us know how wonderful and blessed we feel when we receive something we have always wanted or something that turns out to be of enormous benefit to us. Jesus seeks to give us new insight into a greater blessedness. It is blessed to receive, but it is more blessed to give! Today, give by showing someone some love!

~~~~~

Prayer

Generous God, I am thankful for all that you have blessed me with. Teach me the joy of giving. Fill my heart with your giving Spirit and use me to unselfishly give to benefit others. I trust that as I give, I will discover that giving is the greatest blessing. I pray this in Jesus name, Amen.

Love Note 17

"...choose you this day whom you will serve (King James Version, Jos. 24.15b)."

Someone has said that today is a gift from God. That is why it is called the present! Indeed, today is a gift from God and the way we live this day will be our gift back to God. So, choose whom you will serve today. Will you serve the God who woke you up this morning and has given you a day that you have never seen before? Or, will you seek to live this day in a way that pleases God and blesses others? It's your choice. Regardless of how others decide to live this day, you have a choice to live it for God. How? One way is to choose to find a way to serve someone else. To serve others, especially those who are the most vulnerable, is to serve the Lord. Perhaps you can start your day by praying a prayer, asking God to give you an opportunity to make a difference in someone's life. Then, prayerfully go throughout the day and let the Lord lead you to be a blessing to someone. That's a good way to serve the Lord. Try it. Now, go out there and show someone some love.

~~~~~

Prayer

Lord, today I choose to serve you. Help me to live with integrity, compassion and love. Send me opportunities to be a blessing to others and then open my eyes to those opportunities. Lead me so that I will know who to serve and how to serve them. I thank you in advance for the privilege to serve. In Jesus name I pray, Amen.

Love Note 18

"...the one who is in you is greater than the one who is in the world (1 Jo. 4. 4b)."

One of the great joys of being a follower of Jesus is the promise of the indwelling presence of the Holy Spirit, sometimes referred to as the Spirit of Christ. This means that the same one who was raised from the dead abides in you! If indeed Christ has conquered sin, death and the grave and now lives in you, then you have the power to deal with anything the enemy brings. Life is difficult, the devil is busy, but Jesus is greater! So today, do not live in fear of what may happen. Do not stress over the possible struggles of today. Do not become distracted by any obstacles you may have to face.

Whatever the day brings, there is one within you who is greater than anything that can be against you. Walk in the confidence and courage that comes from knowing that because of the one who is within, you are ready for anything! With this faith, go out and show someone some love.

~~~~~

Prayer

God, I rejoice in your abiding presence in me. Thank you for the gift of your Holy Spirit. I walk in confidence today because your Word reminds me that a greater power resides in me than the enemy who lurks in the world. I can move through this day with courage, confidence and faith because the power and presence of your Holy Spirit in me guarantees my victory! In the mighty name of Jesus I pray, Amen.

Love Note 19

"Do not be anxious about anything, but in everything, by prayer and petition, with thanksgiving, present your requests to God (Phil. 4.6)."

Don't worry, pray! That is essentially what the verse for today is admonishing us to do. We are encouraged by the Word of God not to approach the challenges of life by worrying. Worrying adds nothing positive to your situation. It is not useful or beneficial at all. Worrying is not constructive; it is destructive. The good thing is that worry is not the only response we have to the stresses and struggles of life. There is a better way than worry. Paul tells us that instead of worrying, pray! We worry because we take life's concerns all on ourselves. But when we pray, we learn how to give it all to the Lord. Take everything to the Lord, large and small, and lay it before God. In fact, Paul adds that we ought to do it, "with thanksgiving"! I suspect that we ought to do it with thanksgiving, not only in gratitude knowing that we don't have to handle it alone, but also in anticipation that God will handle it! What a blessed truth! God loves you enough to do that for you. In light of that love, go out today and show someone some love!

~~~~~

Prayer

Gracious Father, forgive me for the sin of worry. Deliver me from worrying by teaching me to take everything to you in prayer. I know that I don't have to handle life alone; so, I pray about all that I am challenged with in life and I do it with confidence and thanksgiving! In Jesus name I pray, Amen.

Love Note 20

"And the peace of God, which transcends all understanding, will guard your hearts and your minds in Christ Jesus" (Phil. 4.7)."

As an alternative to worry, Paul has admonished his readers to pray! Paul says that we ought to take our concerns to the Lord in prayer, trusting that God is willing and able to help us. In light of that truth, Paul then declares that when we give our struggles and stresses to God in prayer by faith, the result will be that we will begin to experience a strange kind of peace. Paul calls it, "the peace of God." This peace cannot be manufactured by human effort. Peace is supernaturally imparted. When we trust God with the things of life that are too much for us, Paul maintains that God's peace will stand guard over our heart, not allowing it to be disturbed by anxiety and worry. God's peace "transcends understanding." In common vernacular that means that God's peace "just don't make no sense!" That's bad English, but it's expresses a sound theological truth: to experience the peace of God, you must have peace with God. Give your heart and life to Christ today and experience God's peace and love. Now, go out today and show someone some love!

~~~~~

Prayer

Lord, I praise you that when I bring all of my issues and cares to you in prayer, that you not only handle them all, but in exchange for them, you will grant me your peace. Hallelujah Lord, for your peace that surpasses all understanding. Today I claim that peace and walk in the peace. In the name of the Prince of Peace I pray, Amen.

Love Note 21

(2 Co. 9.7b "...God loves a cheerful giver)."

Someone has said that we are no more like God than when we give. All through the Bible, we are called to be people who give. We are to give especially to those who are the least fortunate. Today's verse reminds us that what is important about giving is not only the act of giving but also the attitude with which we give. God loves it when we give cheerfully! When we give with an attitude of joy, we mirror the very heart of God! Who wants to receive a gift given with a grudging heart? That's like giving a steak to a hungry man served on a garbage can lid. What is given is nice, but the delivery leaves something to be desired. Let's be givers, but let's give with a joyful spirit! People may see the hand that gives, but God sees the heart! Today, let's give by showing someone some love!

~~~~~

Prayer

Giving Lord, thank you for all that you have blessed me with. You are so gracious and kind to me. And, as I give to the Kingdom and to those in need, please give me an attitude of gratitude. Teach me to rejoice in giving, thankful that I have something to give and that what I give, you can use to bless others and glorify Your Name. In Jesus name I pray, Amen.

Love Note 22

"The Lord is my shepherd, I shall not want (Ps. 23.1 KJV)."

These are among the most well-known words in all of the Bible. Most recognize these words as the declaration of David who sings of the wonderful care of God. If David wrote these words in the sunset of his life, he is looking back on his life with God and is singing of how God has cared for his life just as a shepherd cares for his sheep. This idea was precious to David because he was once a shepherd and he knew with what great care a true shepherd took care of the sheep. David is testifying in song that through all of life's ups and downs, God has provided all that he has ever needed. Followers of

Christ can testify of the same. God can and will take care of you. God never promised that we would not have some hardships and hard times, but the God we serve is willing and able to provide for all of our needs. Today, walk in the blessed assurance that God will provide whatever you need. As you walk in the assurance that God will provide, go out today and show someone some love.

~~~~~

Prayer

Caring God, I thank you for your loving care. Through the ups and downs of life, even in seasons of disobedience, you have always been there to lovingly provide. My heart is full of gratitude for your faithful care. I love you more than I can say. In Jesus name I pray, Amen.

Love Note 23

"...our God whom we serve is able to deliver us...
(Da. 3.17b KJV)."

Today's scripture emphasizes the deep and profound confidence that three Hebrew boys had in the power of God. They had been threatened with being thrown into a furnace stoked with fire if they did not bow down and worship another God. They refused to bow down. They were loyal to the one true God and were confident that He was able and willing to deliver them from their fate. This kind of faith is impressive and inspirational. This kind of faith invites God to the fight. This kind of faith sets the stage for a miracle. I wonder what would happen if we lived each day knowing that whenever we are threatened by people or circumstances to bow down and compromise our loyalty to God, if we stand firm on our convictions, our God is able to deliver us. Indeed, God is able. God has delivered before. God can do it again. God is that kind of God. Stand up for what is right and remain faithful to God no matter what. God might show you a miracle that will not only deliver you, but glorify God and cause others to trust in God, too! Go out now, on behalf of a God who delivers, and show someone some love.

~~~~~

Prayer

Strong and able God, there is none like you. You have come, over and over again, to my rescue in times of threats when I stood for you. Continue to give me the courage to stand up for you no matter what the cost, knowing that you are able to deliver me. This I trust. In Jesus name I pray, Amen.

Love Note 24

**"But if not...we will not serve your gods...
(Da. 3.18 KJV)."**

Three Hebrew boys had just fearlessly declared
that they would not bow down and worship
another God because they believed that their God
was able to deliver them from the threat of being
thrown into a furnace filled with fire. Their
rationale was that they believed that their God
could and would deliver them. That was admirable
in and of itself, but our text today reveals a deeper
kind of loyalty. It is one thing to serve God if you
believe He will get you out of every tight spot and
preserve you from all harm, as long as you remain
faithful to Him. It is another thing for these

Hebrews to show that they are loyal to God because of who God is not just because of what God is able and willing to do! That is true faithfulness. Mature faith is faithful to God because of the relationship, not simply because of safety, security, or some understanding that God will keep you from all harm or danger. Faithfulness is trusting God even if it costs! When you love God for who God is and not simply for what he can do for you, then you are faithful to God, regardless of the danger, cost, shame or inconvenience. Let us pray that we have the Hebrew boys kind of faithfulness. Be faithful today and go out and show someone some love.

~~~~~

Prayer

Strong deliverer, I know that you are able to deliver me from any and every attack, trial, or test when I stand for you. Still, if you do not deliver me from the trouble, give me courage to stand and endure for your name sake. I desire that you get glory from my life

whatever the cost. I want to do right because it's right to do right, regardless of the price. I pray that you grant me grace to live with that kind of faithfulness to you. In Jesus name I pray, Amen.

Love Note 25

"Filled with compassion, Jesus reached out his hand and touched the man...the leprosy left him and he was cured (Mk. 1.41-42)."

There is power in the human touch. In the text, Jesus reached out and touched a man whom no one else was willing to touch. Compassion prompted him to do so. There are many things that Jesus did that perhaps we will never do, but there is one thing we can do...we can reach out and touch someone in some helpful and healing way. Jesus specialized in touching or influencing the lives of people who others would ordinarily shy away from. The outcasts, the despised, the rejected in society were often on the top of Jesus' list. Jesus was willing to reach out to them, prompted by compassion rather than condemnation, and their lives were transformed. They were never the same again! I wonder what would happen if we dared to be like Jesus. I wonder what would happen if we, starting today, would reach out to someone who is isolated, alone, picked on, left out or hurting and touched them with some meaningful act of love and compassion. Could it be that one touch of compassion from you could actually begin to alter someone's life? If we would touch the hurting with a touch of love, perhaps they would be open to hearing about the Jesus who one day touched us with love that forever transformed our lives. Go out and touch someone by showing them some love.

~~~~~

Prayer

Lord, one day you compassionately touched my life and I have never been the same. Teach me to reach out and touch others with love, especially those who are

rejected, isolated, excluded and alone. Fill my mind with wisdom so that I will know how to minister with your mind and fill my heart with your compassionate spirit so that I can be your instrument of care and transformative love in the world. In Jesus name I pray, Amen.

Love Note 26

"Do whatever he tells you (Jo. 2.5)."

These words are connected to the miracle of Jesus turning water into wine. The wine had run out at a wedding feast. Mary, Jesus' mother, went to Jesus with the crisis. She did not know how Jesus was going to remedy the situation, but she gave some wise counsel to the servants at the wedding. She told them to, "Do whatever he tells you." Sometimes we make discipleship more complicated than it really is. Following Christ and living with him as Lord, means a lot of things. But one thing it means for certain is that we have to trust him enough to do whatever he tells...,us. This word is especially meaningful when you are in the midst of a crisis like they were in the text. If you read the story in its entirety, you will discover that sometimes what Jesus tells you to do may not make sense to you; but if you trust Jesus, then trust his word. You will discover that the Word of the Lord can be trusted. Trust the Word of the Lord and go out today and show someone some love.

~~~~~

Prayer

Dear Lord, teach me to trust your Word. Forgive me for those times when I trusted my own ways above yours. If you are Lord of my life, and you are, then I will treat you as such by trusting you enough to do whatever you say. I know you have my best interest at heart, so your Word is my guide. In your precious name I pray, Amen.

Love Note 27

"For God so loved the world that he gave his only begotten Son that whoever believes in him shall not perish but have everlasting life (Jo. 3.16)."

This verse is by far among the most cherished verses in all of the Holy Scripture. One author has referred to it as, "the gospel in miniature," because it has housed within its brief words the sum and substance of the whole of the gospel message. It speaks of the love of God for all of humanity. Notice how it characterizes God's love. God does not just love the world, but God "so" loved the world. God loves us with an intense love. God loves us with a love so intense that God was willing to give His own unique Son, Jesus Christ, so that we might have the gift of eternal life. He died so that we might live. What a wonderful God we serve! If God is willing to give us such a marvelous gift, we should never doubt His love for us. God withheld nothing good from us. God gave us His very best! God's best for us ought to inspire our best for God and the best we can do for God is to love God and our neighbor as ourselves. Do this and we honor God's great love for us. Now, be grateful enough to go out and show someone some love.

~~~~~

Prayer

Loving God, thank you for your precious love. Only your love saves. It is in awe and with profound thanksgiving that I receive your love in Jesus Christ. The gift of your Son to me is better than life, indeed; it is life itself and I rejoice in that love. Your love is so incredible that I can't keep that love to myself. So Lord, I pledge to share the message of your love with others so that they can know your redeeming love. In

the name of Christ I pray, Amen.

Love Note 28

"The tongue has the power of life and death... (Pro.18.21 KJV). "

How will you use your tongue today? Speech has influence and words have power. The way we use our tongue is critical. Our words can be used to build up or to tear down, to help or to hurt, to cut or to heal, to make bitter or make better, to kill or to make alive! There is power in our tongue. God desires that we use our tongue for His glory. Our tongue is best used to bring life to those around us. Our conversation should be such that we bring out the best and not the worse in those who are in our company. Our words have such power that what we say to others can help make them great achievers or great disappointments. Our words can encourage a soul who is tempted to quit or empower one who may be weak and struggling. Who would you want to have around you when you are trying to accomplish something meaningful in your life - someone who is constantly telling you why you will fail or someone who is convincing you that you can succeed? The challenge today will be to use your tongue, indeed your speech, to add what is good and subtract what is bad from the lives of those around you. Remember that old adage, "If you can't say anything good, then don't say anything at all!" Now go out today and use your speech to show someone some love.

~~~~~

Prayer

Lord, thank you for the gift of speech and the power of words. With words you brought order out of chaos, hurled worlds into existence, and created life. Since I am made in your image, teach me to use the

power of my tongue to do the same. Teach me to use my words to bless and not curse and to bring light, life, and order where there is darkness, death and disorder. In Jesus name I pray, Amen.

Love Note 29

"She said to herself, "If I only touch his cloak, I will be healed (Matt. 9:21)."

The text for today reports how a woman was healed from an embarrassing flow of continuous bleeding she had suffered from for 12 long years. She had spent all the money she had on physicians and was not only completely broke, but her condition had become increasingly worse. She heard one day that Jesus was passing by, so she made her way to see Him. What is striking in the text is that one of the strategies she used to get her to the source of her healing was self-conversation – "she said to herself." Yesterday we dealt with the power of speech toward others. But what is equally important is how you talk to yourself. The woman in the text was motivated toward a miracle. In the face of overwhelming odds, she chose to encourage herself with powerful, purifying, and empowering self-conversation. She kept saying encouraging words to herself until she reached her goal: to touch the cloak of Jesus. When her hand touched what her faith reached out for, she discovered that He had a hospital in His hem and she was immediately made whole, all because she knew how to talk to herself. The truth is, there are going to be times in your life when the only words you can depend upon are your own. Learn how to talk to yourself in a way that believes that you can when all around you says you can't. If no one will talk to you the way you need, then learn how to talk to yourself! Now, today, tell yourself to show someone some love.

~~~~~

Prayer

Dear Lord, teach me how to speak to myself. Teach me to speak words of life, power, affirmation and faith to myself. Let my self-conversation contain words that build up, strengthen and empower my spirit. Most of all, let me speak to my own heart truth of your love and acceptance of me so that I can declare your love to others. In name of the Word made flesh I pray, Amen.

Love Note 30

"And he went a little further... (Matt. 26.39a)."

Jesus has taken his disciples to the garden with him to pray. He left them at a certain place to pray, but then the text reports, "And he went a little further." These are arresting words. The great Samuel Proctor, reveals how these words not only describe the fact that Jesus went deeper into the garden to pray, but the words are, in a real sense, a commentary on his life. Jesus was in the habit of going a little further than others and a little further than what was expected. In fact, some concluded that He would, at times, go a little too far. He not only ministered to sinners, but actually ate and fellowshipped with them. He didn't just speak to lepers, but He even touched them. He not only spoke well of women, but He allowed them to accompany Him, along with the male disciples. He didn't just die for His friends, He also died for His enemies, for the Bible teaches that, "While we were still sinners Christ died for us"(Romans 5:8). Since we are His disciples, we are called to live like Him and to go a little further, too! We are not to just love our friends but we are called to love our enemies and those who persecute us (Matthew 5:44 NIV). If we are going to make a difference in the world for the sake of the Gospel, we cannot be satisfied with simply doing what others have done. We have to be like Jesus: surprise the world and be willing to go a little further. Go a little further today and show someone, preferably someone who does not deserve it, a little love.

~~~~~

Prayer

Dear Father, I thank you that your Son went a little further and died on Calvary for my sake. I never want

to be a disciple who only does just enough. Let me live like your Son and go a little further in love and service to others. In Jesus name, Amen.

Love Note 31

"Take courage! It is I. Don't be afraid (Matt. 14.27)."

Jesus' disciples are in a boat on a storm tossed-sea, straining to stay afloat. No doubt they are threatened and troubled by the wind and the waves. Right in the midst of the storm, Jesus comes walking on the water, declaring words of comfort and encouragement. The Lord wanted them to be encouraged by the fact that He was with them in the storm. They should have been encouraged since He was walking on the water, which meant that what was threatening them was under His feet! No one goes through life without His share of storms. With the inevitability of storms is the invincibility of Christ! Jesus has power over the external storms of life and can bring peace to the internal storms of the human heart. When the storms of life come, know that no storm can keep the Lord from you and that when He appears, He is greater than any storm! Go through the day encouraged by that truth and show someone some love.

~~~~~

Prayer

Master of wind and waves, I am comforted and encouraged by the fact that you are always with me, even in the storms of life. It is the reality of your guaranteed presence in the storms of life that gives my heart peace and my soul comfort. Today I walk in faith and not fear, knowing that you are present and powerful in all my storms. In the name of the Lord of storms, Amen.

Love Note 32

"Then Peter got out of the boat, walked on the water and came toward Jesus (Matt. 14.29)."

Peter has just made a mind-boggling request of Jesus. He asked Jesus if He could walk on the water in the midst of a storm with Him. Jesus invited him to "come" and Peter got out of the boat and walked on the water! Astounding! It is incredible enough that Jesus is walking on the water. What is more astounding is that Peter is walking on the water as well! That ought to be encouraging because we have more in common with Peter than we do with Jesus. If Jesus can teach Peter to walk on the water, with all of His flaws, faults and failures, then He can teach us to walk on the water, too! That is the power of this passage. Jesus can teach us how to master our emotions and exercise our faith in the midst of storm tossed situations in our lives. Jesus can teach us to take what used to frighten, intimidate and control us and put it under our feet! Isn't that a blessing? We do not have to live as victims of circumstances. We can master our circumstances with the correct inner-stances. Jesus can teach us to walk by faith, master our emotions and make progress even in the midst of a storm. Armed with that truth, live with courage today as you go out and show someone some love.

~~~~~

Prayer

Master, teach me how to be a water walker. Show me how to live without being ruled by surrounding circumstances. Give me courage to get out of the boat knowing that while it may be safe in the ship, it's exciting on the sea. Lord, as long as you are out there on the water with me, I'll take the risk and learn to walk on the water, even in the teeth of the wind. In

your strong name I pray, Amen.

Love Note 33

"Lord, save me. Immediately Jesus reached out his hand and caught him (Matt. 14.30b-31a)."

Peter had the extraordinary experience of walking on the water with Jesus, but distracted by the wind and waters around him, he takes his eyes off Jesus and begins to sink. Peter cries out for help and Jesus immediately reaches down and saves him. There will be times in our lives when we exercise our faith, and being obedient to Jesus, step out on faith and begin to accomplish some incredible things. This faith pleases the Master, but the truth is, there may also be times when while we are in the midst of our faith walk, that we become distracted by what is happening around us. Things like the winds of public or personal criticism or the waves of intimidating circumstances may cause us to take our eyes off Jesus. When those times come, remember that Jesus is near. Call out to him and he will reach down and grab you by the hand and keep you afloat. Indeed, He can lead you back to the place of safety. Our Lord knows that we will have moments of doubt and fear, but sinking is not the worst thing. What is worse is never having the faith to get out of the boat! Keep trying to be like Jesus, get out of the boat and dare to walk on the water. Today, while you are exercising your faith, be sure to show someone some love.

~~~~~

Prayer

Jesus, today I will not be afraid to walk on the water. I focus my faith and put my trust in you today no matter what happens. If I happen to become distracted by my situation, I will cry out to you, believing that you will rescue me and take me back to the place of safety.

Today I am not afraid. Today I trust you and try. Today I take the first step. Today I get out of the boat. Today I walk on the water. In your name I pray, Amen.

Love Note 34

"Father, give me... make me (Lk. 15.a19b)."

In the well-known parable of the prodigal son, the younger son is preparing to leave home to go to the far country, far from the loving care and covering of his Father. As he prepares, he selfishly utters the words "Father, give me..." This self-centered attitude characterizes his predominate disposition. He cares nothing for the Father, his rules or his feelings. All he wants is what the Father has for him so that he can go and squander his inheritance away. Unfortunately, so many relate to God the same way the prodigal son did. We believe that God is only good for what we can get from Him. We care little for His love, plans or purposes for our lives. We know what's best, not God. So we trust ourselves, take what He provides and selfishly squanders it all in reckless living. "Give me" - That is the way the son spoke while he was leaving home, as he was moving away from his Father. Notice how the son speaks when he returns home. His speech is not "give me," but "make me"! It is this second expression that reveals that the son has truly come to himself, for his words represent the best desire that can be expressed by a child of God. Not "give me," but "make me." Now the son does not simply want something, he wants to become something. It is good to know that God is the source of all that we want to possess, but greater still is the knowledge that God is the source of all that we can become! More than giving you something, God wants to make you someone. His best gift to you is to give you your best self in Jesus Christ! Let this be your dominate ambition and predominate prayer – "Father...make me!" As you surrender to that ambition, go out and show someone some love.

~~~~~

Prayer

Benevolent Father, forgive me for loving the blessings you give more than I love you. Forgive me for wasting both the things you have given me and the life you have blessed me with. Forgive me for thinking that it is better to "have" than to "become." Lord, more than anything else, I want you to make me what you want me to be. So, today, my prayer priority is not "give me," but "make me." In Jesus name, Amen.

Love Note 35

"But one thing I do... (Phil. 3.13b)."

Few things are more powerful than a focused life. When a life is focused, that life has a tendency to order all energy and activity around the "one thing" it aspires towards. That life has a tendency to attract all those things that have a tendency to assist in reaching that goal or accomplish that one thing it aspires. With great intensity, it moves because it creates greater force. Like water forced through a small opening, it spurts with greater force than when that same water is dispersed through a greater opening. When one can find the one thing and focus on it, then one has won half the battle. The Bible says elsewhere, "A double-minded man is unstable in all of his ways." But not a focused person. Focus brings power and focused power, when focused toward a particular direction for a particular purpose, is not easily stopped and can accomplish great things. What is the focus of your life? What do you plan to focus on today? If you can find that "one thing" today, you will find yourself organizing your day and prioritizing your life around that one thing. If you do that, you might be surprised by what you accomplish. While you are moving throughout the day, find a spot to show someone some love.

~~~~~

Prayer

Dear Lord, I dedicate this day to you. As one who seeks to be a good steward of my life, I desire that this day be focused and productive. Give me discernment to know what that one thing is that I should dedicate my energies to today. Help me to prioritize my day so that I will stay focused on that one thing and not be distracted or deterred. I pray that the power of that focus will attract the resources needed to accomplish

what you desire for me to accomplish today. I praise you ahead of time for the accomplishments of this day. In Jesus name I pray, Amen.

Love Note 36

"Forgetting those things which are behind... (Phil. 3.13b)."

The way to true freedom and spiritual progress is learning what to do with your past. You cannot change the past. Omar Khayyam was correct when he penned the grim words in his poem, "Rubaiyat." "The moving finger writes, and having writ moves on; Nor all your piety nor wit shall lure it back to cancel half a line; nor all your tears wash out a word of it." What is done is done. The past cannot be visited or revised. However, the past can be reflected upon and learned from, but never allow yourself to become a prisoner of your past. We must learn how to let the past stay where it belongs – in the past! We must have creative amnesia. We must forget the past, releasing it so that we can be free to claim our future. We can never really go forward until we learn to let go of the past. Anything in the past that threatens to hold you back and trip you up, let it go. Let go of past pain – what others have done to you. Let go of past mistakes – what you may have done to others and even to yourself. Release them to your history so that you can claim your destiny. Accept God's forgiveness in Jesus Christ. Then forgive yourself. Release the weight of guilt and shame and receive the cleansing power of the love of God and the blood of Jesus Christ. Now, let God give you wings to fly beyond yesterday into tomorrow! Today, as you take flight into the possibilities of this day, show someone some love.

~~~~~

Prayer

Holy God, thank you for the gift of this day. Today I release the past to the past. All mistakes, mishaps, and mess-ups, I leave behind me. Today, I receive the

liberating power of your forgiveness and walk into the freedom of today's possibilities. No longer encumbered by yesterday's failures, I seek the grace to maximize each moment that today brings. Thank you for a brand new day. In Jesus name I pray, Amen.

Love Note 37

"...straining toward what is ahead, I press on toward the goal to win the prize for which God has called me heavenward in Christ Jesus (Phil. 3.13b-14)."

Spiritual progress not only requires that we let go of the past, but simultaneously, we should reach forward toward our God-ordained future. While releasing ourselves from the past, we must reach relentlessly toward our future. You were created to move forward. In fact, your very anatomy is a clue that you are meant for forward movement. Everything about you physically faces forward. Your eyes look forward, your nose points forward, your mouth is made forward, your ears tilt forward, your head points forward, your arms, hands, legs and feet are all directed forward. In fact, the only thing about you that faces backward is that part of you intended to eliminate what you don't need so that you can move forward better! You are created to make progress. In the passage chosen today, Paul paints the portrait of a runner literally leaning forward, every muscle straining, while the whole self is reaching ahead. This, for Paul, is the picture of what the Disciple's disposition should be toward spiritual maturity. We should invest all of our spiritual might and total selves to letting go of anything that hampers us and reach toward anything that helps us reach the heavenward goal of becoming all that the Lord desires and has designed for us to become. This process and growth never ends. But there is a level of maturity you reach that prepares you for the deeper things of God. It is in reaching forward toward the call of God on your life, that your life becomes deeper, richer, more fulfilling, clearer and more empowered. The character of Christ is carved out in you and you learn to live, love, and serve with His heart. That is a miracle! That is living! Today, lean forward and reach for your destiny. When the chance comes today, show someone some love.

~~~~~

Prayer

Gracious Lord, I thank you today for an exciting future in Christ Jesus. I claim the future you have for me, one full of purpose, power, growing faith and spiritual maturity. Strengthen my faith so that as I run my race, I can lean forward into my future with all of my might. Today, I run knowing that that progress is both forward toward spiritual maturity and upward, reflecting the high standards of godly living. Today, I run to become a little more like Christ. In Jesus name I pray, Amen.

Love Note 38

"If I make my bed in hell, behold, thou art there (Ps. 139.8 KJV)."

In this Psalm, the writer celebrates the omnipresence of God. God is everywhere. But those of us who receive that truth by faith sometimes forget that "omnipresence" means everywhere at all times. We often make the mistake of thinking that God is only present and available in good times. To be sure, it is a blessing to know that God is with us when all is well. But the wonderful truth about our wonderful God is that God is present even in the worst of times and situations. God is not only present in the sunlit summer days of life, but God is right there when we are in the teeth of the winds of life's brutal storms. In the lowest places of life, in hell, God is there. God's love will not allow God to abandon us at the times when we need Him the most. All believer ought to take to heart that God will never leave us nor forsake us. We have the promise of his constant cosmic companionship. God is not like some people in our lives. God is not a "fair-weather friend." God is not with us when things are good and gone when things get bad. God is forever present and prepared to grant us the benefit of His presence, if we would face every situation by faith, knowing that God is present, even in hell. So, the next time you are going through a hellish situation, know that God is there! In fact, you may be in hell now. If that be true, know this: regardless of how you feel and no matter how things look, behold, God is there! Trust God. God can see you through. Today, walk in the power of the knowledge of his presence. Today, as you live strengthened by that loving presence, show someone some love.

~~~~~

Prayer

Ever present God, thank you for the gift of life, but life can be hard and harsh sometimes. Sometimes it can be a living hell. But I take courage in knowing that you, oh Lord, are with me when life is at its worst. I know that when life is at its worst you are at your best! So I trust and lean on you always, because you are always with me no matter what life brings. Today I am not afraid. No matter what happens, your presence is enough. In your precious Son's name I pray, Amen.

Love Note 39

"Follow me, and I will make you... (Matt. 4.19)."

When Jesus was choosing His initial disciples He would often call them by saying, "Follow me." This was His personal call to be His disciple. While it was a great privilege to follow the Master, it was no small matter. The life to which He calls a disciple is not only a life of joy and peace, but it is also a demanding life. It is a life that the flesh often rebels against. That is why the Master also said that we are to "take up our cross" and follow Him. The cross still stands for death. It stands for crucifying the old and putting on the new. But what is glorious about following the Master is that He not only offers a costly invitation, "Follow me," but He also makes an exciting promise, "...I will make you..." Housed within these words is the realization that even though the call of Christ on our lives is demanding and far beyond what we can fulfill on our own, Jesus never expects us to do it on our own. He calls us and promises to make us what He is calling us to be. In the text, Christ promises to make His disciples "fishers of men" and by the power of Christ, that is what they would indeed become. In fact, when we yield to His leading, we can become "fishers of men," too. Even larger than that, we have His Holy help to become all and everything He wills for us to become. We can rejoice in the fact that our Lord and Leader does not call us to live and serve without making us into what He has called us to be. Praise the Lord! As we surrender daily to the influence and teaching of the Master, we will indeed become just what He wills. He will shape, fashion, cut, carve, make and mold us into the Christ-like disciples that He wills and that we desire to be. Hallelujah! Today, seek and surrender to the leading of the Lord and let Him make you more and more like Him. As part of the process, go out today and show someone some love.

~~~~~

Prayer

Dear Lord and Leader, I praise you for saving me and then calling me to be your disciple. Today I surrender afresh to the influence of your Spirit. Your strength and grace will help me meet the demands of obedience. Your goodness and power will help me be a useful follower in the kingdom enterprise. You've been good to me, now be good through me so that others will know of your love. In your precious name I pray, Amen.

Love Note 40

"Be still, and know that I am God (Ps. 46.10)."

When one reads the admonition in this verse, one might get the impression that the Psalmist is advocating that we be physically still. But, in fact, the emphasis of this admonition has less to do with our physical position as with our inner deposition. To "be still" really means to let your hands hang down, to relax. It means to release the tension of anxious anxiety and to rest. So many times we allow ourselves to become anxious about our lives and the circumstances and situations we have to face. But it is useful to hear the words of this Psalm afresh and trust God enough to just relax, to cease working frantically in nervous insecurity and go limp, if you will, and relax in the Lord. What helps us learn to relax and rest in the Lord is what we know of the Lord. God is God! We know what that means because we have read about God in the Bible and because we have a history with God ourselves. We know God personally. So in a real sense, we are encouraged to let our hands drop to our sides rather than frantically try to handle everything on our own because God has proven, repeatedly in our lives, that He is able and that we are not in the world alone. God has not left us to fend for ourselves. We can count on God to help us; indeed, our God is able to handle anything, so we can...relax. We can be emotionally, mentally and spiritually still and rest in our very strong God. Today, rest in God and while you rest, show someone some love.

~~~~~

Prayer

God of power and peace, you know how anxious I can become at times, especially when things are out of my control. But today your word reminds me that I can

rest in you. At any given time, things may be out of my control, but they are never out of yours. So Lord, I vow today to learn to relax, to let my hands hang down. You are God, so I don't have to be. In your capable name I pray, Amen.

Love Note 41

"Taste and see that the Lord is good (Ps. 34.8)."

When it comes to knowing the goodness of the Lord, today's verse is a personal invitation for personal investigation. If you want to know for yourself, then you must see for yourself. This is sound advice. When it comes to knowing the Lord, you should never simply take someone else's word for it. The wonderful thing about the Lord is that you can have your own personal relationship and experiences with God. Once you have your own relationship with the Lord, then like the Psalmist, you will feel compelled to invite others to know the Lord for themselves. You will be convinced that they will also discover that the Lord is good. God is good because goodness is God's nature. Because good is what God is, then good is what God does! The Bible says that God is the giver of all good and perfect gifts. That's because God is good. It is important to know that this invitation is an open invitation. God is no respecter of persons. Indeed, the Lord desires that all would come to know Him and experience His goodness and grace. Take the risk and get to know God today. If you already know the Lord and have experienced that the Lord is good, then make it a point, when opportunity provides, to invite others to see for themselves just how good our Lord really is. Encourage them to take a risk and try God for themselves. They will find that the popular saying is true: "God is good all the time and all the time God is good!" Now, in the name of a good God, today, show someone some love.

~~~~~

Prayer

God, there is none like you. Your goodness is sweet

like honey in the honey comb. I have tasted of your wonderful goodness through your Son, Jesus Christ. Every day with you is sweeter than the day before. Hallelujah! Give me the opportunity and today I will share the good news of your goodness to someone so that they too may taste and see that you are good! In your sweet name I pray, Amen.

Love Note 42

"Behold, I stand at the door, and knock: if any man hear my voice, and open the door, I will come in to him, and will sup with him, and he with me (Rev. 3.20 KJV)."

This is a request from the living Lord Jesus Christ to have access to and fellowship in the human heart. It is moving to read of a Savior who loves so deeply that He will take the initiative, come to us and request an audience, indeed access and fellowship with the likes of us. But that is what He does in this verse and that is what He does daily. Imagine the Lord standing on the outside of your heart, pleading for you to let Him in so that you can have a relationship with Him. It is the Lord's desire to have an ever-increasingly, intimate relationship with all who will open the door. Notice that the Lord stands at the door and knocks. He does not kick it down, nor does He sneak through any windows. Even though we need the Lord more than anything else, He is a polite Savior who respects the dignity of our freedom to choose. He does not impose Himself on us in order to force us to love Him because love is not coercion and coercion is not love. The Lord wants us to let Him in voluntarily, so that means the door is locked from the inside. We must open and give Him access. Yet, if we are to be true to the context of the text, these words from our Lord are not words to unbelievers. They are applicable to unbelievers; but the verse is really the words of our Lord spoken to the church. It is a word to believers. If that is the case, what is the Lord doing on the outside knocking on the door? Could it be that believers are sometimes guilty of becoming so preoccupied with the things of the world that we end up crowding the Lord out of our lives until at last He ends up outside, begging to come back in? Could this be a scripture about restoration? If so, then here we have the Savior begging those of us who believe to restore a neglected relationship with Him. Before you start the day, examine yourself and see if the Lord is where He ought to be in your life. If not, let Him back in and begin to experience the joy of restoring your relationship with the lover of your soul. Now live today walking in that joy and showing someone some love.

~~~~~

Prayer

Lord, I praise you for loving me enough to initiate a relationship with me. Forgive me for becoming so preoccupied at times with the cares and responsibilities of life that I crowd you out. Today, I begin by opening up any area of my life that I have closed off from you. My whole life is open to you today. Enter in and come close. I am yours. In Jesus name I pray, Amen.

Love Note 43

"After this I looked, and there before me was a door standing open in heaven. And the voice I had first heard...said, "Come up here, and I will show you what must take place after this (Rev.4.1)."

These words are recorded as part of the apocalyptic vision of the Apostle John. Caught up in the spirit, he has already heard what the Spirit had to say to the seven churches in Asia Minor. Now it appears that the Spirit of God wants to show John things that are to come. The message that John receives in the remainder of the book is astounding. But there is something we should notice about the invitation extended to John by the voice of the One who speaks to him. The voice says, "Come up...and I will show you..." The voice reveals to John that there is more to be seen and experienced. There is more to witness. There is more that the Lord desires for John to see and know. But notice the subtle prerequisite: "Come up here..." It is almost as if the voice is saying to John that although there is more that I want to show you, you can't see it from where you are, so you must "come up here." It is true to human experience that sometimes in order for God to show us what He wants to show us, we must first "come up" in our living. We must move a little higher in our walk with God. "Low down" living can not give up high revelation. We must come up! What are the areas in your life that need to come up? Could it be that there is much more that God wants us to see, understand, and experience, but our living is not high enough? Are our lives being operated on the high plain of moral integrity? Are we governing our lives, decisions, businesses, marriages and other relationships according to high ethical standards or moral excellence? Perhaps God is using this verse to challenge you to live higher this year so that He can show you things you have never seen before and take you places you have only dreamed of. Start today to take your life higher in God. Do it and watch God start to work. Start today by showing someone some love.

~~~~~

Prayer

Lord of vision and revelation, I long to see what you desire to reveal. Teach me to walk in your ways. Empower me to take the high road of Christian living so that I can see with spiritual insight what you want me to see. Forgive me for those places and spaces in my life that are morally low, do not honor my relationship with you, and therefore steal divine vision from my life. Today, I commit to live at the level you are calling me. Let me see what you desire to reveal. In Jesus name, Amen.

Love Note 44

"Therefore I tell you, do not worry...

(Matt. 6.25a)."

These are the words of Christ from his famed Sermon on the Mount. With compassion, He admonishes His hearers to learn to live without worry. That admonishment might have seemed strange to the persons He was teaching, given that they were living on the lower end of the socio-economic ladder. They might have responded to him by saying, "As bad as things are for us, we have reasons to worry. We have a right to worry." I dare say that there are many people in our time who feel the same way. Things may be tight for them or times may be difficult. When life is filled with struggles and uncertainty, people often conclude that it just makes sense to worry. The future is so uncertain; it's just normal and even sane, according to some, to worry about the things of life. But in the face of it all, Jesus says don't worry because the Lord loves you and will take care of you! If He clothes lilies of the field and feeds the fowls of the air, surely He will provide for you who bear His image! Jesus is not saying that we should not have constructive concern about the future. He is saying that we should not have destructive anxiety about the future. Plan for, but don't worry about the future. You may not know what tomorrow holds, but remember who holds tomorrow! God loves you and will take care of you. Now walk in the certainty of that love by showing someone some love today!

~~~~~

Prayer

Dear Father, I thank you that you care about your children. I confess that there are times that I worry about tomorrow. Forgive me. Thank you for

reminding me in your word that if you care for flowers and fowl, you care for me. I will prepare for tomorrow, but I will not worry about what I have no control over. If I can trust you to keep my soul in eternity, surely I can trust you with tomorrow. Today, worry is not on my agenda. In Jesus name I pray, Amen.

Love Note 45

"Am I now trying to win the approval of men, or of God? Or am I trying to please men? If I were still trying to please men, I would not be a servant of Christ (Gal. 1.10)."

One thing is for sure, the Apostle Paul was not a people pleaser. He lived completely for the approval of the Lord. There is a kind of liberty to having your highest allegiance to the Lord. When pleasing and obeying Him is our top priority, we are less likely to be susceptible to the desires and expectations of the world. When we can live ultimately devoted to the Lord and His claim and call on our lives, then we are uniquely postured and positioned to best be used by God. We can be leaders instead of followers, originals and not copies, headlights and not tail lights, voices and not echoes, ambassadors and not imposters. We are free to follow the leading of the Lord, rather than being easily conformed to the pressures of our culture and times. This means that a disciple of Jesus has to be willing to stand for the Lord even if he or she has to stand alone. But if our highest allegiance and deepest dedication is to the Lord, His will and His way, then we consider it a delight to stand for His cause.

When we consider what the Lord has done for us and the great price He paid that we might be set free and inherit eternal life, it is a small matter to stand up for Him. Gladly will we stand up for Him and even suffer for His name. Love and gratitude compel us to make serving the Lord our top priority. So today, let us dedicate ourselves afresh to the Lord. And as we seek to faithfully serve Him today, let us be sure to show someone some love.

~~~~~

Prayer

Lord, forgive me for those occasions when I am guilty

of being a people-pleaser. There are times when I am seduced into caring more about pleasing people than pleasing you. I am your disciple and I am sold out to you. I will serve others and bless others, but I will seek to please only you. Today, I claim the freedom that comes from being totally yours. Use me in any way you choose. In your precious name I pray, Amen.

Love Note 46

**"Make a joyful noise unto the Lord, all ye lands...
(Ps. 100 KJV)."**

On this day of worship, we embrace the call to worship housed in this verse. Today we give praise to our great God. We dare not keep quiet. As the Psalmist declares, we make "noise unto the Lord." The noise we make is joyful. We praise God for who God is and what God has done. We praise God because we are filled with joy at the wonder of our God! Without shame, hesitation, or reservation, we open our mouths today and praise God's Holy Name! God is our creator and our sustainer. Like a shepherd cares for his sheep, God supplies all of our needs. God has blessed us throughout this year and throughout our lives; so, we enter the sanctuary and bless God in return! We praise God for God's goodness, for His unfailing mercy, and because His truth endures! But most of all, we praise God for God's radical love shown to us in God's son our Savior, Jesus Christ! Our hearts explode with thanksgiving and gratitude at such an unspeakable gift. Let all the lands rejoice with us today as we lift Holy hands, open our mouths, sing, testify, pray, preach and celebrate our creator, redeemer, sustainer and lover of our souls! And don't forget, after the benediction, show someone some love.

~~~~~

Prayer

Precious Creator, I praise you today for you who you are. You are the great "I Am," the Eternal One. You are love and justice. You are compassion and Truth. You are active in time and greater than eternity. I praise you for what you have done. You bless, heal, transform, enlighten, deliver, and set free. I praise you most of all for your Son, my Savior and Lord, Jesus

Christ, without whom I would not enjoy eternal life, Amen.

Love Note 47

**"And there was evening and there was morning...
(Genesis 1:5, 8, 13, 19, 23, 31.)."**

The verse we have chosen is a common phrase that shows up six times in the book of Genesis in the creation story. Each day that God creates, the end of the day is marked with the phrase, "And there was evening and there was morning..." This phrase is the characteristic way that the writer measures the days. He signals that each day has ended with this phrase. It seems such an innocuous phrase, but it is really quite instructive. In contemporary time, we measure the days differently than the Genesis account does. We measure our days starting with the morning and ending with the evening. The evening signals that the day is over, the end has come. But notice that the Genesis account measures the days by starting with evening and ending with the morning. The morning signals that the day has ended. The day ends with the morning and not the evening. It ends with the day and not the night! I wonder what would happen if we started measuring our days and times and circumstances the way the day is measured in the book of Genesis. What would happen if we ended with the day and not the night? That would mean that the day would not be over until the morning came! What a useful principle to guide our lives. Instead of giving up when times get dark, we should remember that it's not over until the morning comes! We can't quit when it's dark because we are quitting too soon. According to Genesis' way of reckoning time, it is morning, not evening, that has the final word. So after every night, just know that morning is sure to come. You may be in a dark place right now but hold on, morning's coming! Maybe you can help someone make it until the morning by showing them some love.

~~~~~

Prayer

Lord of the morning, I praise you for the fact that darkness does not have the last word. Sometimes I am tempted to become depressed, anxious and overwhelmed when times are dark and difficult. But I am reminded that it is the morning that has the last word. Light, love, and truth have the last word. So today I will not give up because things are tough. Today, I will rejoice because I know whatever I am going through, it ain't over until the morning. In Jesus name, Amen.

Love Note 48

"The Lord is with you, mighty warrior (Jdg. 6.12)."

These are an angel's words and God's assessment of a man named Gideon. The interesting thing about these words is that there seems to be no indication in the life and behavior of Gideon to suggest that he was anything like the title he was given. Up to that point, he had not shown any evidence that he was a "mighty warrior" at all. In fact, at the time these words were uttered, Gideon was in hiding from the enemies of his people. He was the least person, in the least family, in the least tribe among an oppressed people. But despite his lack of status, his fears, and his severe lack of self-esteem, God called him a mighty warrior. And, indeed, Gideon becomes just what God called him.

God has the power to call those things that are not as though they are because He knows He has the power to make them what He calls them. Gideon may not have looked like much when God first addressed him, but by the time God finished working on him, he would be a great leader and liberator. God has this holy habit of looking past the surface of a person's life and seeing deep within their possibilities. He does not judge a person based on what they are presently, but on what they can become potentially. If you dare to trust God with your life, God's perfect hands of influence can make and mold you into a great man or woman of God. The same hands that hung the worlds in space can do things with your life that will surprise you and those who think they know you! No matter what your life has been up to this point, today, hear the Lord calling out the best in you. Hear God saying to you, mighty man or woman, that you are more than the failures of your past or the negative circumstances of your present predicament. You are His great warrior! Today walk in that truth.

Now, go and show someone some love.

~~~~~

Prayer

Dear Creator, thank you for believing in me. Thank you for looking beyond my failures and seeing my possibilities. I give myself to you afresh today to use me as you see fit. Take what I am and make me what you want me to be. I am not a defeated, worthless nobody, no matter what my circumstances are. I am mighty in you. Help me walk in the victory you have declared in Christ. In Jesus name I pray, Amen.

Love Note 49

"Put on the full armor of God, so that when the day of evil comes, you may be able to stand your ground, and after you have done everything, to stand (Eph. 6.1)."

Warren Wiersby, Pastor, teacher, and writer of Christian literature, reminds us that the Christian life is not lived on the playground, but on a battle field. The enemy has declared war against God, God's people and all that God stands for. But we are not helpless against evil or evil's schemes. We are not without the means to fight and fight effectively. Paul instructs us to put on the armor of God in order to do battle against the wicked ways of the evil one. If we are dressed properly, we may not be able to avoid the battle, but we will be equipped to fight with confidence. With the whole armor of God, we can stand courageously at our post, knowing that our armor is more than enough for the onslaught of the enemy. When the dust settles, we will still be standing.

Notice that Paul writes that we should put on the "whole" armor. If we ignore the totality of what is needed to fight, then we go to battle ill-equipped to win. To fight with armor missing is to leave oneself dangerously and unnecessarily vulnerable to attack. So make sure that you dress for battle in full battle gear. When we do this, we prove that we are more than conquerors through him who loves us! Trust the armor for it is ideal for successful spiritual warfare! Tomorrow we begin to look at the armor. Today show someone some love.

~~~~~

Prayer

Strong God, I know that I am in a fight with the enemy who is the prince of this world and with the enemy

that is in me! But you have given me what I need to fight and win. By faith I put on the whole armor you have provided and expect the victory! I am more than a conqueror in Christ Jesus! Today I fight to win! In the name of the Lord Jesus I pray, Amen.

Love Note 50

"Stand firm then, with the belt of truth...

(Eph. 6.14a)."

I believe that it is no small matter that Paul mentions "the belt of truth" before he mentions any of the other armor parts. The belt is worn around the waist and is central to the stability of much of the armor. Without truth, everything else falls apart, for truth is fundamental to the fight against evil. It is truth that the enemy wants to make the first casualty in the fight. It is no accident that Satan is known as the Father of Lies. And while lies may seem to flourish at times, it is truth that is eternal. Someone has said that lies travel fast because they know that they don't have long to live. Consider the famous quote from Martin Luther King, "Truth crushed to the earth will rise again." No life can survive and thrive without truth being central to its existence. And even though so often it seems that truth lay prostrate on the streets of society and lies have the upper hand, James Russell Lowell wrote, "Truth forever on the scaffold, wrong forever on the throne, yet the scaffold sways the future and behind the dim unknown standeth God within the shadow keeping watch above his own."

Truth always wins in the end; so, as we fight the good fight of faith, let all that we do be rooted in the Truth. Let us do everything with integrity and let us live trusting in the Truth of God's Word. If we live led by Truth, we can win in every area of life. Let the belt of Truth hold everything else together. As we live committed to truth today, let us show someone some love.

~~~~~

Prayer

God of Eternal Truth, today I enter battle against lies

without and within by putting on the belt of truth. What is truth? Your Word is truth. So I hide your Word in my heart so that I will not sin against you. And if I do sin, the truth is, you will forgive me. I commit to honoring you by living with integrity in everything that I do today. I know that as I stand on truth today, I stand on a firm foundation. In the name of the one who is ultimate truth I pray, Amen.

Love Note 51

"...with the breastplate of righteousness...

(Eph. 6.14b)."

In Jesus' day, the Roman soldiers wore a breastplate that covered the vital organs of the soldier, like the heart and such. It was important when a soldier went to fight that he always had on his breastplate. Paul, speaking of spiritual warfare, names the breastplate of righteousness as one of the pieces of armor for the Christian soldier. This piece is important because righteousness is a characteristic of the disciple of Christ. One of the weapons that the enemy will use to undermine the power and confidence of the believer is the one that questions the authenticity of the believer's salvation. The ammunition the enemy uses is the fact that even though you claim to be saved, you still sin in your life. With this knowledge, the enemy will attack your heart. He will seek to take away your enthusiasm for Christ and question Christ's love for you or your love for Him. He will taunt you by suggesting that if you really loved the Lord you would not be so weak and sinful. And then he will seek to destroy your confidence by claiming that you are not really saved and safe and accepted by God. Ultimately, he will seek to cause you to question whether you will spend eternity with the Lord in an effort to get you to live in fear and anxiety. But the devil is a liar, and we must be prepared to guard our hearts against the lies of the enemy with the breastplate of righteousness. It is important to note, however, that righteousness for the Christian is first of all a gift from God through Jesus Christ. Our own behavior is never good enough to earn us salvation. Our righteousness alone, the Bible says, is as filthy rags in God's sight. But Jesus lived a perfect life and gives us His righteousness in exchange for our sinfulness. "He, who knew no sin, became sin so that we who are sinners could become the righteousness of God in Christ." We stand before God righteous, not because we have been perfect, but because we have surrendered our lives to Christ and by faith have received the perfect righteousness of Christ. But now that we are declared righteous by the blood of Jesus, we are called to live a righteous life. We are called, by the aid and assistance of the Holy Spirit, to live a life of righteousness, so the world will see the difference in us and give God the glory. Let the world see how different we are in Christ today by showing someone some love.

~~~~~

Prayer

Gracious God, thank you for righteousness that comes to me as a free gift through Jesus Christ. This truth protects my heart from the accusations of the enemy. I can walk in confidence, knowing that I am

accepted by you, flaws and all! So, because of the gift of your righteousness, I am inspired to live a life of righteousness, not to earn favor, but out of gratitude! Thank you Lord. In your righteous name I pray, Amen.

Love Note 52

"And with your feet fitted with the readiness that come from the gospel of peace (Eph. 6.15)."

Paul includes shoes as part of the equipment of the Christian soldier who is to be successful at spiritual warfare. When one puts on his shoes, it signals that he is ready to move. The shoes of the soldier in the army of the Lord signal that we are to be ready to move, anxious to go out and share the good news of the gospel of Jesus Christ! Every day we must be prepared to take advantage of every opportunity to share the gospel with anyone who would appear open to hearing and accepting it. The shoes are also significant in another way as well.

The shoes of a Roman soldier had knobs on the bottom of them to give the soldiers traction for sure-footing. It was to give them stability on any terrain. It was to make the soldier sure- footed. In our warfare with the enemy, we have to be sure - footed, standing firmly on the promises of God and the certainty of the gospel of Jesus Christ. The enemy will try to trip you up by making you second guess the certainty of your salvation and the promises of God. As the lyricist, Edward Mote wrote, "On Christ the solid rock I stand all other ground is sinking sand." Standing on Christ, the gospel, and the Word of God puts every believer on a firm foundation in the midst of the struggle against the wiles of the enemy. Know that in Christ you are saved and know that you can trust in the promises of God. The Bible says that God is not a man that He should lie. If we are going to be able to stand in the struggle against the enemy, then we have to make sure that we put on our shoes. Now, with those shoes on, go out today and show someone some love.

~~~~~

Prayer

Lord, thank you for gospel shoes of readiness! Thank you for a spirit that is ready to share your gospel as I am going throughout my day. I realize that the enemy will seek to deter me, but I stand on your promises and the sure footing of certainty that they provide deep in my soul. Today I walk in confidence because of the shoes! In Jesus name I pray, Amen.

Love Note 53

"...take up the shield of faith, with which you can extinguish all the flaming arrows of the evil one (Eph. 6.16)."

Faith is fundamental to what it means to be a believer. We cannot hope to fight the good fight without faith. The Bible says that, "Without faith it is impossible to please God." And the great Charles Adams said, "Without faith it is impossible to please God because without faith it is impossible to have God." Both the Old and New Testament declare that, "The just shall live by faith." Paul refers to "the shield of faith." The Roman soldier had a long oblong shaped shield that virtually protected the entire body. One of the lethal weapons used by the enemy was an arrow or dart soaked in pitch and set on fire. The enemy would shoot these flaming arrows at the soldier who would shield himself against them by holding the shield between himself and the arrows. The arrows would hit the shield and then go out. In spiritual warfare, the enemies seeks to defeat us with fiery darts of temptation, lies, doubts, and fears to cause us to fall. The enemy seeks to use these things and more to cause us to fall away and disobey our Lord. But faith is complete trust in Christ; so, if we walk close to Christ then we can be protected from the power of temptation. Then we can stand! So, have faith in Christ! Today, walk by faith in the finished work of Christ and the power of his word and stand firm against the wicked one. As you walk the walk of faith today, be sure to show someone some love.

~~~~~

Prayer

Dear God, I know that faith is the key to victory.

Today, I choose to walk trusting in you and your word. By faith I face every challenge that comes my way today. I know that faith is the master key that unlocks the door to your unlimited power, so my greatest weapon against the enemy is faith. My faith is not in faith. My faith is in you! In Jesus name I pray, Amen.

Love Note 54

"Take the helmet of salvation... (Eph. 6:17a)."

When we go to warfare with spiritual wickedness, we have to be sure to cover our heads. Paul says our head is covered by the "helmet of salvation." Satan wants to attack our minds. That is where the battle is really fought. The Bible says, "As a man thinketh so is he." It is important that we have the correct mindset when we do battle with evil. We are to be transformed or changed by the renewing of our minds. Satan will try to attack our minds with his lies, but we are to cover our heads with the truth about our salvation and the truth of God's Word. Faith convinces us that we are saved and forgiven, past, present and future. So we take this certainty into battle knowing that we can fight with the confidence that we belong to God forever! Guilt and shame do not weigh us down because we know that we have been forgiven. The helmet also is a reminder that we need to grow in the knowledge of the Lord. We are to bring our minds to the battle. We are to love God with heart, soul, mind and strength. The more we know, the more we can grow in the faith and the stronger we become as soldiers in the fight against the lies of the devil. Do not let the enemy "get in your head." Do not let the enemy influence your thought life. Commit your mind to the Lord. Let the truth of God's Word infiltrate and influence your mind and it will protect your thinking from the lies of the enemy. Today, we celebrate the certainty of our salvation and walk in that power. Today, we commit our mind to be used by the Lord so that we can think God's thoughts after God. Today, we pledge to study God's Word daily and fill our mind with the cleansing power of His word. Someone once complained that "Christianity ain't nothing but brainwashing," to which his Christian friend responded, "Well, if there is anything that needs washing, it's our brains." Have a mind to serve God today and show evidence of it by showing someone some love.

~~~~~

Prayer

Heavenly Father, I thank you for my mind. I am grateful that I am saved and I am thankful for the certainty of my salvation. Today I surrender my thought life to your influence. Today I protect my mind with your Word. Today I love and serve you with my mind as well as my emotions and will. Teach me to think your thoughts after you by trusting the influence of your Spirit. In Christ's name I pray, Amen.

Love Note 55

"...and the sword of the Spirit, which is the word of God (Eph. 6.17b)."

One of the most potent weapons that God has given us for spiritual warfare is God's Word. The word of God has power to defeat the evil one. Even when Jesus was tempted by the devil in the wilderness, He used the word to win against him. At each encounter with the enemy, while in the wilderness, Jesus responded to the enemy's attacks by saying, "It is written." If the sinless Savior won by using the word while here on His earthly sojourn, then surely you and I can benefit and indeed win by using the word. In fact, Paul refers to the word as, "the sword of the Spirit." What a powerful image. It is the truth of God's word that gives us the ability to stand against the schemes of the enemy, knowing the Word helps us win the battle. The Word is our defensive weapon against the attacks of the devil and our offensive weapon against the evils of the world. It's a two edged sword! A physical sword cuts the body, but the spiritual sword cuts to the heart. A physical sword hurts; the spiritual sword can heal. The trials, tests and troubles of the world and the attacks of the enemy are only temporary, but the word of God is eternal. "The grass withers and the flowers fade, but the word of God shall stand forever (Isaiah 40.8 ESV)." You can depend on God's word! Don't go to battle without knowing, living and relying on the Word of God. The enemy will not be defeated by "I think," or "I feel," or "My opinion is..." But the enemy can be defeated by "It is written"! Line up your life with the Word, and as you live it out today, show someone some love.

~~~~~

Prayer

Eternal God, I thank you for keeping your word throughout the centuries so that I can have a guide for my life. Your word is a window through which I can see your truth and a mirror in which I can see my life. Today, your word will be a "lamp unto my feet and a light unto my pathway." Most of all, God, thank you for your Son Jesus, the eternal logos, who is the Word who became flesh! He is my liberator, leader, role model and inspiration for everyday living. Hallelujah for your Word! In Jesus name I pray, Amen.

Love Note 56

"And pray in the Spirit on all occasions with all kinds of prayers and requests (Eph. 6.18)."

The battle cannot be fought and successfully won without this last ingredient. Once we have put on the armor, we need permanent access to power. The work that we do in the world is the work of the Lord. But we can't do the Lord's work without the Lord's help. The marvelous thing about spiritual warfare is that it has given us the gift of prayer. This discipline is perhaps among the most powerful, but underused weapons, in the Christian's spiritual arsenal. Too often, prayer is relegated to special occasions or just emergency situations. But prayer is meant to be used just as the Apostle Paul has prescribed ..."on all occasions with all kinds of prayers and requests." Prayer is not something that we just tack on to our lives when needed. Prayer is to be intimately and intricately woven into the fabric of all that we do. Prayer is to the spirit what breath is to the body. And if we don't breathe, we won't live. If we don't pray, we can't make it. Prayer moves God, changes things, and even changes the pray-er! There is power in prayer. We cannot defeat the enemy and successfully engage the enemy on our own, but thank God for prayer! Prayer invites God to the fight. And if God be for us, who can be against us? As you put on your armor and as you engage the enemy, don't forget to pray "on all occasions with all kinds of prayer and requests." Jesus faced the cross with prayer. Let us follow His example and face the challenges of life with prayer. Now, go out and show someone some love.

~~~~~

Prayer

God, thank you for the gift of prayer. I thank you that

you always hear me when I pray. I praise you that I can have an ever increasingly intimate relationship with you through prayer. And I am grateful that I can always pray, anytime, anywhere. Teach me to always have my heart tilted toward you and pray without ceasing. Prayer reminds me that I am never alone and that you are always available. Lord, I love you. In Jesus name I pray, Amen.

Love Note 57

"And my God will meet all your needs according to his glorious riches in Christ Jesus (Phil. 4.19)."

What a word. Can you believe this? If you can, you will have discovered one of the secrets to peace and power. This admonition from Holy Scripture are words spoken to the church at Philippi. They had been instrumental in supporting Paul while he served and suffered for the sake of the gospel. In fact, there were times when the Philippian fellowship had remembered Paul when all of the other churches had forgotten all about him. They had been generous in their giving. And Paul assured them that God was not only pleased with their giving, but He would supply all of their needs. It's almost as if Paul was assuring the church that in the midst of their giving, they were not to fret about giving so much that they would not have enough. God will supply.... Isn't it good to know that we can rely on our God to supply what we need? I can't help but wonder if this is especially true for those who seek to give to the cause of the gospel.

God is in the habit of supporting those who support godly causes. A generous people will be generously blessed. Notice that Paul does not say that God would supply their needs according to their needs. Paul declares that God would supply their needs according to His glorious riches in Christ Jesus! The supply would not be determined by the need, but by the limitless abundance of God's supernatural supply. Our need is never greater than God's supply! Take heart today and know that God is willing and able to provide! Go out today knowing that God loves you enough to provide for you and show someone some love.

~~~~~

Prayer

Gracious and generous God, I praise you because you are the source of all that I need. You are able and willing to supply all of my needs. You may not supply all of my "greeds," but you will supply all of my needs. I am convinced that you can supply all of my physical, spiritual, emotional and material needs. I rejoice that you are my reliable source. Teach me to be generous, too. In Jesus name I pray, Amen.

Love Note 58

"Rabbi, who sinned...that he was born blind? Neither this man nor his parents sinned...but this happened so that the work of God might be displayed in his life (Jo. 9.2-3)."

Jesus and his disciples came upon a man who was born blind. Immediately Jesus' disciples seek to assign blame. They wanted to know whose fault it was that this man was born blind. Jesus sees the same man, but does not interpret his situation the same way. Jesus does not see this man's suffering as occasion to assign blame, but instead, as an opportunity for the man's situation to be improved and for God to get glory! The disciples focused on the question, "Who is to blame?" while Jesus focused on, "What are we going to do about it?" Same situation, two different perspectives. One approach majors in judging, while the other approach majors in helping. Could it be that Jesus is teaching us, His disciples, that when we see people hurting or suffering that our primary concern should not be to place blame but to alleviate the suffering? After all, which one do you think God gets the most glory from? Too often we get caught in the paralysis of analysis when we come upon suffering and hurting people, wondering how in the world they got themselves in such a mess. But we do nothing. However, when we see the hurting and the helpless as people to help and not as simply statistics to analyze, then the world will be impressed by our acts of compassion rather than our capacity to analyze and God will be glorified! Maybe our first inclination to those who are suffering is simply to offer a helping hand. Today is a good day to start. Go out today and show someone some love.

~~~~~

Prayer

Compassionate God, please help me to see suffering people through your loving eyes. Forgive me for those times when I looked upon the suffering with self-righteous contempt instead of compassionate concern. Fill my heart with the love of Christ so that I will seek to bless rather than blame. Deliver me from being a professional critic and make me a prolific problem solver. Teach me to be more like Jesus so that when I see suffering people, rather than simply having an opinion, I will have a heart. In your loving name I pray, Amen.

Love Note 59

"And as they went, they were healed... (Lk. 17.14b)."

Ten lepers approached Jesus and asked that he have mercy on them. They wanted to be healed of their disease and knew that Jesus could heal them. Amazingly enough, Jesus simply tells them to go show themselves to the priest. Back then, whenever a leper showed himself or herself to a priest, it was usually because they had been healed and the visit was for the sake of official verification. The strange thing is these lepers had not been healed yet. In fact, there is no sign at all that anything had changed regarding their condition. And yet, Jesus told them to go to the priest. It is almost as if Jesus was telling the ten lepers to behave as if they were already healed even though there was no sign of their healing. The ten did just as Jesus had commanded and the Bible says, "...as they went, they were healed." What a powerful message! It was not until they exercised faith and obeyed Jesus, even though there was no sign of healing, that they were healed.

Note, it was in their obedience, not one second before, that they received an answer to their request. Sometimes we don't see results to our prayers because we want to see it so that we can believe it. But the truth is some things you don't see so that you will believe; you believe so that you will see! By faith, these men were healed and it happened while they were in the process of obeying. "As they went..." they were healed. Perhaps certain things have not changed in your life because you keep waiting on God to do something while all the time God is waiting on you to trust him and obey. Some miracles only happen in your life as you obey the commands of Christ. Some things will only change if we would just obey. Things might change today if we would show someone some love.

~~~~~

Prayer

Lord, I realize that there are times when I am waiting on you to do something when, in fact, you are waiting on me to do something. Teach me how to walk by faith. Show me that if I would just trust and obey that as I am obeying, miracles can take place in my life. Today I trust you and walk in faith, and as I am going I will give you praise! In Jesus' name I pray, Amen.

Love Note 60

"...if you have the faith...as a mustard seed, you can say to this mountain, Move from here to there and it will move. Nothing will be impossible to you (Matt. 17.20)."

Oh the power of faith! That is what Jesus is after in this verse. Jesus is seeking to stir up and stimulate the anemic faith of His disciples. Time and again, Jesus finds Himself frustrated by the lack of faith of His disciples. But here, Jesus seeks to provoke faith in the hearts of His disciples. When Jesus speaks about faith that moves mountains, He is saying several things. First, He is saying that faith is potent. Notice the contrast between the tiny size of the mustard seed and the enormous size of the mountain. Faith is so potent that a little faith in

Christ can move a mountain-sized challenge. But Jesus is not so much advocating mustard seed size faith as He is mustard seed kind of faith. If you take that tiny mustard seed and put it in good ground, and tend to it, let some rain fall on it and some sun shine on it, that seed will get bigger and bigger! So it is with faith. If we take our faith and put it in the soil of human circumstances and let it be tended by the providential hand of God and let some rain fall on it and sun shine on it, our faith will grow and grow and grow and nothing will be impossible to us! Jesus wants us to have developing, growing, maturing faith. And with sufficient faith in the power of Christ we can move any mountain, face any challenge, endure any hardship, accomplish any God-ordained task. As we exercise our faith, with the help of the Lord, mountains will move out of our way! Finally, notice that Jesus declared, "you can say to this mountain...." Jesus says speak to the mountain, not talk about the mountain. Whenever you simply talk about, complain if you will, about anything, it has a tendency to get bigger. But if you want it moved and overcome, then you must learn, by faith, to speak to your mountain. And the more your faith grows, the greater things the Lord will be able to use you to do! Today, exercise your faith by showing someone some love.

~~~~~

Prayer

Faithful God, thank you for faith to meet the challenges of life and do great things in your name. I know that faith is powerful because my faith is in you! So I move through this day equipped with faith that can move mountains! Today I can handle any problem, face any challenge, and transform my situation because of the power of faith! Today I do not despair of mountains. Today I say, mountain get out of my way! In the name of Jesus I pray, Amen.

Love Note 61

"...anyone who has faith in me...will do even greater things than these because I am going to the Father (Jo. 14.12)."

These are probably among the most astounding words ever spoken by Jesus to His disciples. The ministry of Jesus was characterized by extraordinary miracles and the spiritual transformation of people's lives. But as Jesus speaks to His disciples in this verse, He makes the awe-inspiring claim that faith in Him would mean that we, His disciples, would do what He did and even greater things shall we do. Now, how can we do greater things than Jesus? Well, insight comes from a couple of things. First, Jesus emphasizes the place of faith. He declares that if we have faith in Him we can do what He did. So, we must begin by having faith. Do you believe in Jesus? Then trust what He says! Notice also that Jesus rests His claim that we would do greater works on the fact that He would be going to the Father. He was referring to the fact that after His resurrection He would return to the Father. This would be of great advantage to His disciples because He promised that when He left, He would send the Holy Spirit! This is important because while He was on earth in the flesh, He was limited. For example, He could only be in one place at one time, had never traveled outside of Palestine, only spoke Greek, Aramaic and Hebrew – you get the picture. But once He sent us the Holy Spirit on the day of Pentecost, while before Jesus could only be with His disciples, now by His Spirit He could live in His disciples and empower them to do what He could do! He was no longer limited by time and space. He could be in multiple places because He could be in multiple people! Now they could do greater work because they were not only empowered by His spirit to do what He did, but they could literally take the good news all over the world. And they did! They could do greater works because the number of workers and the extent of their work was greater. More people in more places could experience the ministry of Christ through His disciples and experience the transforming power of salvation through the gospel of Jesus Christ! And guess what, as His disciples, we have been given the privilege of joining that number of people who are blessed with being able to do greater things! That is why it is so important to be a part of a church and join other believers in the work of the Lord. We have His power by virtue of His Spirit abiding in us, and we have partnership with other believers so that we can do greater things in His Name, making an impact all over the world! So today, remember that as you serve the Lord, walk in faith knowing that because the power of the Lord is working through you and because you are a part of a larger community of believers, you are doing greater things for the Lord! That is a great motivation for showing someone some love.

~~~~~

Prayer

Dear Lord, thank you for the church and the privilege of serving with other disciples to continue your work in the world. I am excited that by your Spirit, we will be able to do greater things for the Kingdom. I am so grateful to be a part of your movement. Show me what I can do today to further your great work. In your precious name I pray, Amen.

Love Note 62

"And I will do whatever you ask in my name, so that the Son may bring glory to the Father (Jo. 14.13)."

Jesus has declared to His disciples that they would do even greater things than He when it came to the work of the Kingdom. The disciples would be able to do greater things because His Spirit would live in them and they could literally take His power and gospel to millions of people all over the world! So, we as is disciples, will not do greater things in quality, but in quantity! The extent of what we do will be greater than Jesus because we will be able to touch the lives of millions of people throughout the world and in every generation until our Lord returns. But along with that truth Jesus adds an exciting promise. Jesus declares that whatever we ask in His name He would do! That's exciting because in order to do the Lord's work we are going to need the Lord's help. And prayer is access to the power and participation of Christ. So while we are seeking to do Kingdom work, we can ask Christ for anything in His name and He will grant it. Now, it is instructive to note that this is not carte blanche or a blank check when it comes to making prayer request of the Master. The qualifying phrase is "in my name." When we make a request of Christ, the question is can we legitimately make it "in his name"? We cannot ask Christ to do personal harm to someone or make some request that is evil, selfish, unethical or un-Christ-like. What we ask must be consistent with His character and will. That is what it means when Jesus says, "ask in my name." But if you are committed to doing the will of Christ, then it is exciting to know that you can expect to get an answer! Christ will respond so that we are not left to fend for ourselves, under our own steam and strength, as we seek to do the will and work of Christ. When we ask Jesus anything in His name, He will do it! Have faith in that. Now, I am sure it is the will of Christ that you go out today and show someone some love.

~~~~~

Prayer

Lord, participating in the Kingdom cause gives my life meaning and purpose. But I am especially encouraged that your power is available for the work. I rejoice in knowing that I can ask for whatever I need in your name and you will provide. There is power in your name! As I move throughout the day, use my life as an instrument of your love and bring glory to your great Name! In your strong Name I pray, Amen.

Love Note 63

"We are therefore Christ's ambassadors, as though God were making his appeal through us. We implore you on Christ's behalf: Be reconciled to God (2 Co. 5.20)."

One of the great privileges we have as Disciples of Christ is that we are His representatives in the world. Paul refers to us as Ambassadors. This is an insightful term when it comes to the identity and purpose of Disciples of Christ in the world. An ambassador is one who speaks on behalf of another. We, as Ambassadors of Christ, have been given authority to speak on His behalf in the world. Ambassadors speak for another, but cannot speak whatever they want, but must convey the message sent by the country represented. We, as

Ambassadors for Christ, may speak for Christ, but cannot speak what we want, only what we have been commissioned by Christ to speak. That message is in God's word.

An Ambassador serves in another land, but that land is not the ambassador's home. We, as Ambassadors of Christ, serve in this world, but the truth is, this world is not our home. We are citizens of heaven. An ambassador is not financially supported by the land he is visiting. Even though an ambassador may be serving in another land, that ambassador gets support from the land of his citizenship. As ambassadors for Christ, it is good to know that our ultimate support comes from God. God will supply all of our needs according to His riches in glory through Christ Jesus. Finally, if the ambassador dies while serving in another country, he has assurance that his body will be returned home. As Ambassadors for Christ we may die while serving the Lord's cause here on earth, but Paul said, "absent from the body present with the Lord!" The Lord will make sure that we get home! In the meantime and in between time, while we serve as the Lord's Ambassadors here, let us represent Him well by communicating His message correctly, serving Him faithfully and loving all unconditionally. In fact, let's start today by showing someone some love.

~~~~~

Prayer

God, to represent you in the world is my joy. You have been so loving and kind to me that I will represent you without shame or hesitation. Give me grace and wisdom to represent you well. Grant me courage to share your message of truth, love and liberation wherever and whenever I can. May your gospel message through me bring someone to a saving knowledge of you and your transforming love. In the Savior's name I pray, Amen.

Love Note 64

"For me to live is Christ and to die is gain (Phil. 1.21 KJV)."

What Paul describes here is a win, win situation! Paul is declaring that there is a benefit in his living and in his dying, because of his commitment to Christ. There is a benefit in his living because he is in Christ. His chief joy was to live his life for Christ! After all the Lord had done for him, he considered it exhilarating joy to serve the Lord. God had forgiven Paul, saved Paul, chosen Paul and was using Paul for the greatest cause on the face of the earth, and it was all because of God's grace! Paul didn't earn it, and didn't deserve it, but the Lord chose him and was using him anyway. Paul was so grateful and overjoyed that he dedicated all that he had and all that he was to the service of the Lord. He no longer lived for himself, he lived for Christ, hence his declaration, "For me to live is Christ." He was so wrapped up in love and service to Christ that all he did he did for Christ and his Kingdom. Have you stopped lately and considered all that the Lord has done for you? How He gave his life so that you might have life? How He has given you His Holy Spirit to lead, guide and empower you? Have you thought about how God has chosen you to serve in His great cause and supplies all of your needs? Have you thought lately that because He has saved you that you are now an heir to abundant life over here and eternal life in the life to come? What an amazing God we serve! The only reasonable response to so great a salvation and so magnificent a love is to dedicate our new lives to Him! Can you say like Paul "For me to live is Christ." But not only is there benefit in living for Christ, but even if we die, Paul said there is gain! That's because for the believer death is not death, it is departure to a better place. To be absent from the body is to be present with the

Lord! Death does not have the last word for the believer. Christ's resurrection has turned a dead end into a thoroughfare! In our relationship with Jesus, if we live, there is joy in His service and if we die, there is joy in His presence! It's a win, win situation! Live or die, if we are in Christ, we win! With that joy go out today and show someone some love.

~~~~~

Prayer

Oh Lord, I thank you for your Son Jesus Christ because in Him I have abundant life in this life and eternal life in the life to come! Today, I dedicate my life afresh to serving you. With my mind, body, soul, spirit and gifts I serve you. I am encouraged by the truth that because I live a life totally committed to you, I can't lose. As I live for you there is joy in service. And when I die there is joy in heaven! Either way, I win! Hallelujah! In Jesus name I pray, Amen.

Love Note 65

"I must work the works of him that sent me while it is day, for when night comes no man can work (Jo. 9.4 KJV)."

Here, the Lord Jesus expresses His dedication to being expedient about carrying out the will of the Father in His life and ministry. He well knew that anything worth doing was worth doing now. This is essentially because there is such a thing as a missed opportunity. There are some things that we cannot afford to delay in doing. One song writer wrote that, "Time is filled with swift transition." And I might add that time waits for no one. Jesus, therefore, expresses the urgency of now. He did not waste time. He understood that time was precious and fleeting. And we all know how precious time is because we talk about time the same way we talk about money. We talk about "spending" time doing something or "investing" time in people. Jesus' words have housed within them a powerful message for those who intend to do something meaningful with their lives. If we are to make a difference in the world or make a meaningful contribution with our lives, then whatever we plan to do we had better begin now. Yesterday is a canceled check, tomorrow is not even a promissory note. The only redeemable time we have is right now. As followers of Christ it is incumbent upon us to get busy about the business of carrying out God's plan and purpose for our lives. God wants to do great things with our lives; but, we can not behave as if we have plenty of time to start living, because we really do not know how much time we have. So we ought to make the most of the moments we have right now! It is a privilege to serve the Lord, but we have to do it "while it is day" or while we have the chance. Some things just cannot wait. In fact, there are some things that we need to say to one another before it's too late. Maybe we need to say, "I love you," or "Thank you," or "Forgive me," or "You are forgiven." There are some things we should say or do "while it is day"! Let's start today. A good place to start is by showing someone some love.

~~~~~

Prayer

Dear God, thank you for the gift of today. I realize that I only have a certain amount of time on earth. And I know that this life is not a dress rehearsal; it's the real thing. Forgive me for procrastinating with my life. Teach me and to use my time wisely and invest in the people and things that matter the most. In your Name I pray, Amen.

Love Note 66

"There were so many fish that they had to call other ships to help them (Lk. 5.6-7)."

This verse reports an incident where Jesus helped the disciples catch a great catch of fish. Peter had just loaned his boat to Jesus to use as a kind of pulpit to preach from, because the crowd had been so great that they had almost pushed Jesus into the sea. After using Peter's boat to preach, Jesus instructed Peter to push out some from the shore and let down his net. Peter initially explained that they had already fished all night but had caught nothing. But since it was Jesus who was telling them to let down their nets they would. As soon as they obeyed Jesus and let down their nets, they caught so many fish that they ended up calling for partners in another boat to help them. Even with the help of others, both boats were so full that they began to sink. This verse teaches so much. One thing it teaches us is that you cannot give something to Jesus to use to bless others and Jesus not turn around and use it to bless you. Peter let Jesus use his boat to bless others and Jesus turned right around and used Peter's boat to bless Peter. Note also that the disciples had been fishing all night with no results, but when they did the same work under the direction of Jesus, it was fruitful beyond their expectation. This reminds us that when we seek to be productive without the directives and assistance of Jesus, we are destined to come up empty-handed. But if we would seek to follow the direction and leading of the Lord, the results will be beyond our expectations! There is another important principle that is present in the text. Once the boat that Peter owned was blessed with an abundance of fish, there were so many fish that the abundance threatened to sink the ship. But Peter called to some partners present nearby to share the abundance. Of course, this may be a shadow of the coming abundance of human souls once the church is established. But I want to point out the simple principle that Peter was wise enough to call for help to assist him in handling the abundance that God had provided. Had he been selfish, and refused to ask for help and share the abundance, he would have lost both the fish and the boat! Perhaps the days ahead will be days of great abundance, and in your abundance be sure to show someone some love!

~~~~~

Prayer

Gracious God, I know that you are so kind that you are in the habit of blessing with abundance. As I, by faith, offer my life, resources, and gifts to you to be used as you desire, I know that you have a holy habit of blessing in abundance. When that moment comes, remind me not to be so proud and selfish that I refuse to share or ask for help. I realize that blessings are meant to be enjoyed, but they are best enjoyed when

they are shared. In your wonderful name I pray, Amen.

Love Note 67

"Moses, what is that in your hand? (Ex. 4.2)."

Have you ever felt ill- equipped to do what the Lord has called you to do? Have you ever looked at yourself and what you possessed and then looked at the task that you are called of God to do and concluded that I have nothing to offer? Well, you are not the only one. Moses felt like that. Moses, the great leader and liberator of Israel, almost opted out of answering God's call to liberate his people. But God showed him that he had more going for him than he realized. When Moses worried about whether the people would believe that God had sent him, God asked him, "...what's in your hand?" Moses' response was simply, "A rod." Now, we know what he said but we do not know how he said it. I suspect that he did not see much in that rod, and so he did not think much of that rod. He only saw what he was used to seeing, and he certainly did not see it as being useful for what he was called to do. However, he discovered that he had more than he realized. God gave him instructions on what to do with the rod. Once he used it for the Lord the way the Lord instructed, turned it loose and, therefore, over to be used by God, it turned into a snake. And when he grabbed it by the tail it turned back into a rod again. What was ordinary became extraordinary. What was of traditional means became useful in an untraditional way. What was common became uncommon. What was dead became alive. He had something that he could use in a supernatural way for the sake of God's cause. And it was in his hand all along! He had more in his hand than he realized! He possessed more than he imagined. It took God to show him. Often we are called by God to serve him and we feel as if we have nothing to offer, but it takes God to show us just how gifted we are. If we would take what we have,

DR. F. BRUCE WILLIAMS

no matter how simple or ordinary it may seem, and offer it in the service of the Lord, God will reveal to us that He has already given us more to offer than we can even imagine! Do not discount what is in your hand. Do not compare it to what others may have in their hand. Just like Moses let go of the rod and it became a snake, release what you have into the service of the Lord and watch it become something you have never dreamed! Take what's in your hand today and show someone some love.

~~~~~

Prayer

Lord, I pray that you open my eyes to the gifts and resources that are in my hand. I don't mean to overlook them or diminish their value, but somethings I just have blind spots and I can't see what is right in front of me. And sometimes I hold on to what I have so tightly I never see the full extent of its potential. Give me faith to release them in service to you so that they can be used in extraordinary ways.

Thank you Lord for what's in my hand. In Jesus name I pray, Amen.

Love Note 68

"The Lord who delivered me from the paw of the lion and the paw of the bear will deliver me from the hand of this Philistine (I Sam. 17.37)."

The words in this verse are the courageous and faith- filled words spoken by young David as he prepares to fight the giant Goliath. David is filled with righteous indignation when he sees the giant Goliath taunting the armies of God, causing the soldiers to cower in fear. He announces to King Saul that he is willing to defeat Goliath. King Saul is surprised at his courage, seeing as how David is too young for Israel's army and has no military experience to boot. But while David did not have military experience, he did have a testimony. He was confident that the Lord would give him the victory. First of all because of who God is. God is the Lord of hosts and was more than capable of helping David defeat his enemies. But what David really emphasized is that he had a history with God. David argued that while he was keeping his father Jesse's sheep, a lion and a bear came to attack the flock. David fought both of them and the Lord helped him defeat them both. Since God had helped him with his past challenges, God would, therefore, help with his present challenge. If God did it before, he would do it again. David was not only confident in God's power, he was convinced of God's faithfulness. David had a history with God. God had given him victory before, so he was clear that God would give him victory again! There is nothing like having a history with God. When you have a history with God, God gets a chance to prove to you just how faithful He is. Your challenges may change, but God never changes. What He did in the past, He can do in the present, and in the future! Remember, as you face any challenges today, God is able to help you get the victory. Chances are, if you look back over your life, God has already helped you through some difficult challenges. Then if He did it before, he can do it again! While others may not be confident in your capacity to accomplish something great, let your confidence be in the power and faithfulness of God! With that courage, go and show someone some love.

~~~~~

Prayer

God, often when faced with present challenges I forget to remember what you brought me through in the past. Teach me to be like David and learn to apply the lessons of the past to my present predicaments. You are a faithful God. The circumstances may be different but you are the same God. When faced with today's challenges, I will draw on yesterday's lessons in my walk with you and remember that if you were with me in my past, you will be with me in my present, and even in my future. In Jesus name I pray, Amen.

Love Note 69

"I tell you, open your eyes and look at the fields!

They are ripe for harvest (Jo. 4.35b)."

Jesus has had an encounter with a woman at a well and her life had been totally transformed! She is so excited about the Messiah she runs into town declaring, "Come, see a man who told me everything I ever did. Could this be the Christ?" In the meantime, the disciples have come back from town with food for Jesus. When He tells them He is not hungry they are confused, thinking that perhaps someone else has brought Him food. But He explains that He is no longer hungry physically, because He has been spiritually satisfied. Meeting the woman was the will of the Father and Jesus insists that His meat is to do the Father's will. As a consequence of the testimony of the woman who has been changed by the Master, crowds of people came from the town to the well to meet this man Jesus. As they were making their way towards them, Jesus, perhaps pointing to the coming crowd, uttered the words for our devotional, "...open your eyes and look at the fields! They are ripe for harvest." Jesus was alerting His disciples to the fact that people are ready to hear the good news of Jesus Christ. The harvest is ripe, or in other words, the masses of people are ready and receptive to the good news of Jesus. If ever these words were true they are now. Jesus is calling us to open our eyes as well. He desires that we be perceptive enough to see that there are countless opportunities to share the gospel with people who are more ready than we realize to hear of God's love in Christ. God desires that we be awake to the fact that harvest time is here! We are in danger of missing the season, so fruit is in danger of dying on the vine. The hearts of people are ready. Will you be one who helps the Lord bring in the harvest? Will you seize the moment and be sensitive to the season and take the risk of sharing Jesus with someone today? That is a good way today to show someone some love.

~~~~~

Prayer

Saving God, I confess there are days when I am so busy living for myself that I am blinded to opportunities that are ripe to share your message of love. Open my eyes to the season. Help me to notice that this is a time when people are ready to hear the good news of a loving and liberating Savior who came to save, heal and set free. Fill my heart with your love, so that I will lift my eyes from my personal concerns, so that I can notice that there are people ready to receive your good news. In Christ's name I pray. Amen.

Love Note 70

"She is not dead, she is but asleep (Lk. 8.52)."

These are the words of the Lord and they are a perfect example of how faith talks. Jesus has entered the house of a man named Jairus. Those in the house are weeping and wailing because Jairus' twelve - year -old daughter has died. When Jesus looked at the young girl, He does not come to the same conclusions as the others. They say she's dead, but Jesus says she's sleep. It is interesting how people can look at the same situation and come to different conclusions. The weeping crowd wept because the situation looked hopeless. They could see no possible way of a change. They had resigned themselves to the fact that the girls was dead. However, Jesus defined the situation much differently. They saw her condition as permanent. Jesus saw it as temporary. They saw no hope. Jesus saw hope. They deduce that she has no future. Jesus insisted that she did. People don't have the last word. Jesus does. When faith looks at a hopeless situation, it has an uncanny ability to find hope and possibilities where there does not seem to be any. Jesus had made a promise to Jairus that He was going to see about his daughter while she was ill. Now she has died. However, Jesus is not defeated by what defeats others, and Jesus does not lie. If He said He would deal with it, then He will deal with it. Things may have gotten worse, but sometimes God allows things to get worse just so that He will get more glory when He solves the problem. Sometimes the Lord allows things to really get beyond our control so that when deliverance comes, we will know that it was nobody but Jesus! So, if the Lord has made you a promise, do not be controlled by what you see. Remember what He said! Jesus had not lost His mind when He said the dead girl was only asleep. She was indeed dead; but, Jesus was saying in substance, that since He had the power to raise her up, she might as well have been asleep. He has the power to turn what looks like a permanent situation into a temporary one. And Jesus, against all odds, raised her from the dead. Jesus can do the same for us. Give your dead situations to Jesus and watch Him do the impossible! Take that truth with you today as you show someone some love.

~~~~~

Prayer

God of power and love, I praise you because there is nothing too hard for you! As I seek to live by faith, teach me to trust you with what seems hopeless in my life. Remind me that when something seems dead and hopeless to us that you are still able to raise it from the dead. I want to walk with that kind of faith. And when you choose to do a miracle in my life, I will not only give you the credit but I will also praise your name! All glory and honor belong to you, Lord. In your able name I pray, Amen.

Love Note 71

"After he put them all out... He took her by her hand... the girl stood up and walked around... (Mk. 5.40-42)."

These words are the prelude to a miracle. Jesus had made it into Jairus' house and had come to see about his daughter. He had told those in the house who were weeping for her that she was not dead but asleep. The Bible says that they stopped crying and started laughing. Surely Jesus speaks foolishly. But the next verse says, "After he put them all out..." Imagine that, Jesus actually put the mourning people out of the house. He does this because they were undermining the atmosphere. In order for there to be a miracle Jesus needed an atmosphere of faith and not skepticism and doubt. So, in order for the miracle to happen the people had to go. That is often true in our lives as well. God wants to do some miraculous things in our lives, but in order for that to happen for some of us, some things – and even some people – have to go. Negatives attitudes have got to go. Negative people have got to go. Sinful and disobedient lifestyles have to go. Ungodly habits and practices have to go. Unhealthy relationships have to go. God wants to do some marvelous things in some of our lives, but before that can happen, some things have got to go. Once Jesus put the people out, then the miracle took place. Do you want to see a miracle in your life? Do you want God to be at his best in your life? Do you want things to change for the better in your life? Then perhaps you have some spring cleaning to do. Perhaps there are some things that have to go. But once you give those things their eviction notice, step back and watch God do something incredible. Today can be the start of your breakthrough. Claim what God is going to do in your life. Now, go do something positive in someone else's life. Show someone some love.

~~~~~

Prayer

Lord, I want nothing in my life that blocks your presence, purpose and power. Give me the courage and faith to evict anything from my life and separate myself from anyone in my life that blocks your best for me. I surrender all. Have your way. As I obey, the separation may be difficult and even painful but I also expect a miracle of healing and wholeness to take place. I trust that my life will be the better for it. In Jesus healing name I pray, Amen.

Love Note 72

"We seem like grasshoppers in our own eyes, and we looked the same to them… (Nu. 13.33)."

The people of God stood at the circumference of the city limits of the promise land. They could literally look over and see their inheritance. They had sent 12 spies in to check out the land and to bring back a good report. They all agreed that the land was just the way God had reported. It flowed with milk and honey. But out of the 12, 10 of the spies reported to the people that contrary to what God had told them to do, they could not take the land. They concluded this <u>not</u> because God is a liar. They came to this conclusion because they paid more attention to the way things appeared than to what God said. They saw the riches that God had promised, but they also saw giants in the land. Once they saw the giants, they allowed their fears to short-circuit their faith and decided that it was impossible to take the land. Their fears affected their confidence and negatively shaped their self-image. Consider their words, "We seemed like grasshoppers in our own eyes..." No one told them they were grasshoppers. But because they were controlled by fear rather than faith, they called themselves grasshoppers! Fear distorted their perspective and they developed a grasshopper mentality. Their condition was so bad that not only did they voluntarily see themselves as grasshoppers, but without talking to the giants they saw, they concluded that the giants saw them as grasshoppers as well! They had lost the battle before they even started fighting, all because of fear. God has not destined us to live by fear. God has called us to walk by faith! When you walk by faith, you know in your heart of hearts that God will do just what God said He would do. Just as important, you know that you can do what God says you can do, regardless of how things may look. An entire generation of people missed out on God's incredible blessings, not because there were giants in the land, but because there was fear in their hearts. Don't let that be you. Take courage and walk by faith. "God has not given us a spirit of fear..." Live your life by faith in the promises of God. Dare to dream big. Attempt great things for God and expect great things from God. The promise land is yours if you will feed your faith and starve your fears. Today, begin to walk by faith and you will inherit a destiny and a future greater than your wildest dreams. Go out now and by faith, show someone some love.

~~~~~

Prayer

Gracious God, I do not want to miss out on the destiny you have for me because I am controlled by fear. I know that you have a purpose and a plan for my life. I know that you have a divine destiny for me. I believe

that there is a promised place for me. Teach me to be inspired by faith and not paralyzed by fear, so that despite the challenges I see, I will claim my destiny. In Jesus' name I pray, Amen.

Love Note 73

"But because my servant Caleb had a different spirit and follows me wholeheartedly, I will bring him into the land... (Nu. 14.24)."

Because of their lack of faith, an entire generation had forfeited their chance to enter the Promised Land and would die in the wilderness. Lack of faith made them miss out on what God had promised. But there were two people out of an entire generation who would still be able to enter the Promised Land and enjoy its blessings. One of them is mentioned in our devotional text today. His name is Caleb. While 10 of the 12 spies said that they could not take the land because there were giants, Caleb spoke up (Joshua was with him) and said, "We should go up and take possession of the land, for we can certainly do it." That's faith talk. Faith made obstacles look like opportunities. Caleb had faith in God. And because he believed in God, he also believed in himself, because God was the one who told them to take the land. And even though Caleb got out voted, God declared that because he had a spirit of faith he would inherit the promise. Isn't that something? He was in the same generation as the others, but he ended up with a different future than everyone else. Why? Because he had a different mindset, a different spirit. He believed God. And because he had faith in God, God preserved his future. He may have had to go through the wilderness with others, but because he had faith and a promise from God, He didn't go to the wilderness to die. He would live through it to claim his inheritance. Would you dare to be different from your generation? Do you have the faith and nerve to stand up for God in the midst of an unbelieving generation? Can you say 'yes' to God's promises, even while the majority in your generation is saying 'no'? Can you walk by faith while others in your generation choose to be controlled by fear? Can you do that even if you have to do it by yourself? If you can, then like Caleb, you have a different spirit and because of that, God's future is yours! It is a future filled with God's best. Celebrate that today as you show someone some love.

~~~~~

Prayer

God, give me the spirit of Caleb. Give me the faith and courage to stand in the midst of an unbelieving generation and trust your Word even if I have to stand alone. I want my life to be a testimony of what happens when one trusts in you. I know I have to live in the same world as others, but I don't have to live in it the same way! A different life creates a different future! In Jesus name I ask this, Amen.

Love Note 74

"Give, and it will be given to you. A good measure, pressed down, shaken together and running over, will be poured into your lap (Lk. 6.38)."

As Christians, we are called to live by a different set of values and principles than the world. In fact, if you compare kingdom principles to much of the way the world lives, they are often the exact opposite! One of the things that is often true about this world is that it can encourage people to live an aggressively self-centered life. We are taught explicitly and implicitly to live for self, to take and not give. But the kingdom of God has as its center the very heart of God! And if there is one thing that is true about God, it is that God is a giver. God is supremely generous. God is so generous that He rains on the just and unjust alike. So, to be like God, we must answer the call to have a generous spirit. We are taught by scripture to be open-handed givers and not closed-handed takers. We are called by our Lord to live to give, rather than living to get. When we live a life of giving, we are being like God who was so generous that He gave His only begotten son, who then gave His life so that we might have life everlasting. As Jesus teaches us the way of the giving heart, He reveals to us a wonderful principle of generosity. He declares that if we give, it will be given back to us. That's the way things work. Give to others and God will see to it that others give to you. And although our motive for giving is not so that we can receive, the fact is Jesus is telling us that generous people are rewarded with generosity from others. And it will be "pressed down, shaken together and running over." That's a description of abundance! A godly life is a giving life. And those who live a life of generous giving will be blessed tremendously in return. So, today as you go about showing someone some love, it's coming back to you.

~~~~~

Prayer

Gracious and generous God, thank you for being so good to me and to others. Forgive me for those times when I have been selfish and greedy. Help me cultivate a spirit of generosity and a habit of giving. Purify my motives so that I do not give to get, but that I give out of love and gratitude for all that you have already done. And when I am blessed because I have been a blessing, I will be careful to give you the praise! In your name I pray, Amen.

Love Note 75

"Dear friends, now we are children of God, and what we will be has not yet been made known (1 Jo. 3.2)."

What an exciting word. Because the love of God has been lavished on us, we can be called the children of God. That is what we are right now! Already, we are somebody! We are Kings' kids, children of the Most High. Never let anyone convince you that you are, "a nobody." Don't let your present circumstances convince you that you are, "a nobody," either. Now that you are saved, you are the offspring of the Creator of the Universe. You are a child of our Heavenly Father. And this Father knows how to take care of His children! In Christ, the Bible says that you are part of a Royal

Priesthood and a Holy Nation. You are an heir and joint heir with Christ. You are more than a conqueror. You are the salt of the earth and the light of the world. You are the righteousness of God in Christ. You are the apple of God's eye. So, you are already someone in Christ. You are all the things the Bible says you are. But the scriptures add one exciting detail: "...what we will be has not yet been made known." That means that God is not finished with you yet! As wonderful as it is to be what you are right now in Christ, the best is yet to come. It's going to be greater later! As good as God has been to you, the best is yet to come! You should get up every day with the blessed assurance that your best days are not behind you, they are ahead of you. And the best you is not the present you. The best you is the future you. As you continue to cooperate and surrender to the work of God in your life, you become more and more like Jesus. What can be greater than that! If you're excited about that, then celebrate by showing someone some love.

~~~~~

Prayer

Dear God, I am so excited that I am yours! I rejoice in the knowledge that, through Christ, I am born of your Spirit. I am grateful for what I am right now. But Lord, I am overwhelmed by the thought of what you have in store for my future. I am ecstatic about the fact that my best days are ahead of me. I face the future with tip-toe anticipation, knowing that it has your finger prints all over it! Regardless of what might be going on now, I believe a better future is on the way. I pray this in your glorious name! Amen.

Love Note 76

"We love because he first loved us (1 Jo. 4.19)."

You are loved by God. That is an unimpeachable fact. You are loved perfectly, completely, totally, absolutely, and unconditionally. And you are loved just the way you are. There is nothing you can do to make God love you any more than He does. And there is nothing you can do to make God love you any less than God does. The wise, blessed, and beneficial thing disciples have done is we have received that love by accepting Jesus Christ as Lord and Savior. His life and death on the cross for our sins is the single greatest gift God has ever given to fallen humanity. That divine love is like no other love we have ever known. The writer of John writes that the reason we love is because we were first loved by the Father. So, we can not even brag about loving others, because we only love because God took the initiative and showed us extraordinary love. While we were still sinners living in rebellion against the Father, He poured out His extravagant love on us. What a wonderful God we serve. Having been the recipients of so great a love, we are not only called to love, but we are inspired to love both God and others. The love of God compels us to love others. God's love for us cannot be hoarded; it has to be shared! So today, we seek to love others as God through Christ loves us. Show someone some love.

~~~~~

Prayer

Loving God, I love you. I am amazed that you love me with such a perfect love. Thank you for showing your love by sending your Son to die so that I might live. I know that you command me to love others, but your love for me inspires me to love others as well. By your

grace continue to fill my heart with your love, so that I can love others with your divine love. In Jesus name, Amen.

Love Note 77

"For we are laborers together with God...

(1 Co. 3. 9 KJV)."

Here, Paul reminds believers who we work with and who we work for. We work with one another and together we work for the Lord. This is important to remember because the enemy seeks to create division among believers. It's the old strategy of divide and conquer. The enemy knows that there is strength in unity. So the enemy is always on the lookout for ways to create discord, disunity, and competition, instead of cooperation among believers. One way he does it is by appealing to our ego. If he can get us to compare ourselves to one another - our work, our education, our status, our popularity, what we think we have accomplished -

then he can stir up jealousy, envy and divisiveness. However, we must remind ourselves that although we are made to do different work in the kingdom, we are all on the same level as far as God is concerned. We are a team that God means to work together. Any meaningful results that come from the work we do comes as a consequence of the power of God. Paul reminds us that one may plant and another may water, but only God can bring the increase! We belong to God. The work belongs to God. We are His laborers, tasked with the blessed privilege of being partners with one another and with the Lord in the Kingdom enterprise. We have the opportunity to show that we love God by the love we have for one another. And by doing so, we have a chance to show the world what is possible when a people humbly submit to God and one another to carry out the work of our King. When we do that, perhaps we will inspire someone to want to come to Christ and be a part of this magnificent work of redemption and reconciliation that the Savior is doing in the world. Today, let's hope someone will be drawn to God as we go out and show someone some love.

~~~~~

Prayer

God, from your Word, I am reminded that we are in the work of the Kingdom together with you and with other believing saints. Teach me Lord, to assume an attitude of cooperation and not comparison or competition. Put a spirit of unity in my heart and in the hearts of those within your service. Let our love and unity be a sign to the world that it is possible to live and work together, submitted to your loving Spirit. In Jesus name I ask it, Amen.

Love Note 78

"And who knows but that you have come to royal position for such a time as this? (Est.4.14b)."

These are among the most well-known and insightful words in the Book of Esther. Esther is Jewish queen of Persia during a time when her people are being threatened with extinction. Her cousin, Mordecai, came to her and asked her to use her influence with the king to help save her people. Esther, initially refused to help her people, but her cousin Mordecai reminds her that just because she is the queen does not mean that she will be spared when the extermination starts. Then he inserted the immortal words of our text, suggesting to her that perhaps she has been providentially placed in her position as queen "for such a time as this"? These are powerful words laced with life lessons. For a moment, Esther was guilty of thinking her position of prestige and power was all and only about her. Her cousin had to remind her that there are times when we are given places and positions of influence, not simply for our own personal aggrandizement, but for the purposes of helping others. Sometimes God grants us privileges so that we can be in a position to help those who are underprivileged. God will orchestrate the affairs of our lives so that we can have power, but He desires that we use the power for the powerless. God sometimes grants us prerogatives, benefits, and blessings because God is counting on us to have a mind to use what we have been given to serve those who are less fortunate than us. Contrary to what our culture sometimes teaches, blessings are not all about us. God positions us because He plans on us to have the type of character that does not think more of ourselves, but thinks about serving others. Can you stand to be blessed? Will God's given position and power be used by you to help enhance the quality of lives of others, especially the vulnerable, or will it all be like new wine and go straight to your head? As God blesses you this year with position, power, prestige, advantages, and opportunities, be like Esther and have a mind lifted above your own personal desires and consider how you might use what you have been blessed with to bless others. Perhaps, you can start today by using what you have to show someone some love.

~~~~~

Prayer

Sovereign creator, I know that you are the source of all blessings. Please grant me the mindset that remembers that you give blessings to me so that I can be a blessing to others. When I am blessed, save me from selfishness and help me avoid arrogance. Whichever way you choose to bless me, please give me a spirit that will use my advantages, not only for myself, but for the disadvantaged. In the name of

Jesus I pray, Amen.

Love Note 79

"...by grace you have been saved, through faith - and this not from yourselves, it is the gift of God - not by works, so that no one can boast. For we are...created in Christ Jesus to do good works... (Eph. 2.8-10)."

Paul makes it crystal clear that salvation in Christ is not our doing. We are saved by the grace of God. We have not done nor can we ever do anything that can earn a right relationship with God. So we are not saved by works that we do. Salvation is a free gift of God. But while we are not saved by good works, we are saved for (or to do) good works. That may seem like a contradiction to some but it is not. Works cannot save us, but we are saved to serve. The truth is that there is something terribly wrong if salvation does not express itself in good works. We can never earn what God has given us. However, we are so grateful that God has given us this gift of salvation that gratitude inspires us to want to be worthy of such grace and love. So we are not serving so much out of obligation as much as we are serving out of gratitude. The Bible teaches us the kind of life of service we are called to live. Out of gratitude for the extraordinary gift given to us by our Lord, we seek to live a life of service just like our Lord. We are not saved to sit. We are saved to serve! We commit our lives to a life of service to the glory of God. So, today serve by showing someone some love.

~~~~~

Prayer

Loving Father, I thank you that you sent your Son that I might receive the gift of eternal life. Only by your grace am I reconciled to you. I commit myself afresh to serving you by serving others. I am so grateful for

your mercy that I am moved to show mercy and kindness by serving others in your name. I am created to do good works. Today, for your name sake, I will. In the name of the One who gave His life for me I pray, Amen.

Love Note 80

"After Jesus had gone indoors his disciples asked him privately, 'Why couldn't we drive it out?' He replied, 'This kind can come out only by prayer and fasting (Mk. 9.28-29)."

A man with who had a son possessed by evil spirits came to the foot of Mt. Hermon to get help from Jesus. Jesus was up on the mountain, so the man came to Jesus' disciples to get help, but they could do nothing. When Jesus came down the hill from prayer and fellowship, He came down to His powerless disciples who were arguing with the teachers of the law, who were always looking for opportunities to make Jesus look bad. When Jesus arrived, the man came forward with his possessed son, reiterating to Jesus the problem with his son and the powerlessness of the disciples. Jesus instructed the man to bring the boy to him. Jesus then cast the evil spirits out of the possessed boy in a way that was violent and dramatic, but successful. Later, when Jesus and His disciples came aside privately, the disciples asked Jesus why they could not cast out the evil spirit. Jesus told them that this type of thing can only be successfully dealt with by prayer and fasting. Jesus' indictment against His disciples was apparently that they tried to deal with a mean, stubborn spiritual challenge without being spiritually prepared. What Jesus was referring to was not simply praying and fasting before you handle a problem. What Jesus was really getting at was a lifestyle of prayer and fasting, more specifically, a life lived closed to God. Too often we want to handle serious issues or do effective ministry for those who are hurting, but we do not live close to God. It is not profitable or realistic to wait until a great challenge comes to suddenly decide to fast and pray, and "poof" we have an intimate relationship with God. Fasting and prayer are disciplines designed to help cultivate an ever-increasingly, intimate relationship with God. We cannot wait until the challenge comes to try to get close to God. We should be cultivating that relationship all along. Not only will we be blessed from just walking closely with the Lord, but we will also be spiritually prepared to effectively minister in the Lord's name when opportunities come. Then people will be blessed and God will get the glory. Seek to live close to God so that each day you can show someone some love.

~~~~~

Prayer

Dear Lord, forgive me for expecting the benefits of living close to you without actually doing it. While my relationship with you became immediate the moment I surrendered to Christ, I realize that relational intimacy is never instant. My intimacy with you must be cultivated intentionally over time. Today, I commit myself to the spiritual disciplines I know that work to create an ever increasingly, intimate relationship with you. Those disciplines I don't know, reveal to me and give me the grace to practice them. I long for a closer walk with you. I know you long for one with me as well. Let your will be done, Amen.

Love Note 81

"Not my will but thy will be done (Matt. 26.39, Mk. 14.36, Lk. 22.42 KJV)."

The idea of surrender has negative connotations in our culture. To surrender is to lose, and we do not want to lose. We want to win. So we are convinced by our culture to make sure that we stay in control. We are taught to show no vulnerability. "Don't let them see you sweat." Maneuver and manipulate. Show no weakness and vanquish your enemies. Trust no one and end up on top at all costs. The sad tragedy is that we may follow this formula and end up on top, but also end up frustrated, unfulfilled, confused, guilt- ridden, and empty. But when it comes to discovering the path that leads to life, contrary to the worldly wisdom of our culture, the

Scriptures teach us that the only way to really win is to surrender to God. Jesus lived His life in total surrender to God. He was convinced that God was good, God loved Him, had a purpose for Him, was forever with Him, and wanted the best for Him. So he surrendered everything, always. Because of His surrender, His life split history into B.C. and A.D. His was a life of positive peace, poise, power, purpose, service, meaning and rest. The path to true life is to surrender and trust Christ with your life. True life is not found in cash, cars, clothes, "cribs" or credit cards. They all have their place. But true life is found in the surrendered life. Today, tell the Lord that you surrender. The journey gets tough sometimes because we are trying to sit on the throne of our own lives and take charge of everything, and inadvertently end up fighting against the God who wants to guide and bless our lives. Surrender today. Surrender your past, present and future to God. Surrender your success and your failures to God. Then surrender your hopes, dreams, frustrations, and fears to God. Daily trust the Lord with your entire life, because God can do more with it then you can. Dare to do the opposite of what the culture often demands and learn to surrender all to God. Let go and let God. Having done this, go out and show someone some love.

~~~~~

Prayer

Loving God, today I surrender again. I know that I surrendered when you saved me, but I am guilty at times of taking my life back from you, trusting myself more than you. Forgive me. Sometimes I'm afraid, confused, weak, frustrated or angry. Those are times when I have a habit of taking control and trusting myself and my way, instead of you and your way. I am learning that those are the moments that I should trust you the most. So, today, "I surrender all, all to thee my blessed Savior I surrender all." Amen

Love Note 82

"Trust in the Lord with all your heart and lean not unto your own understanding. In all your ways acknowledge him and he will direct your path (Pro. 3.5)."

God is involved in this world and in the affairs of people. The wonderful thing about the mystery of God's divine involvement is that God is available to be involved in our lives. God has not left us here to fend for ourselves. The Word of God teaches us that God desires to provide divine guidance as we make our pilgrimage through life. God has provided various gifts for us to use as we make important decisions, seeking to navigate through the tests, trials, and temptations of life. We must learn to trust God and to believe that God has our best interest at heart. Then, we must learn to make use of the gifts that God has provided. We have God's Holy Spirit to guide us, for the Bible says that the Spirit will lead us in to all ways of truth. We can consult God's Word for guidance, for it is peppered and punctuated with people and principles that are designed to assist us on our personal pilgrimage. God can use people like friends, family, strangers, and even enemies to guide us as well. Wise counsel from wise and godly people is one of God's great resources for guidance, too. God even uses circumstances to aid us in our decision-making. Sometimes God will use a closed door to detour us and an open door to welcome us. God can guide both our steps and our stops. God guides by providing and by preventing. Do not forget that God has given you a mind to use as well. As we fill our hearts with His love, and our minds with God's Word, our minds become reliable instruments to help guide us as we seek the best for our lives. Finally, a life of prayer is one of our most valuable assets. You can pray regularly to God, but remember, prayer is conversation. Do not do all of the talking. Listen for God as He speaks with you even throughout the day. You are not alone. Make full and creative use of all of the gifts God has provided to help you move through life. Then, by faith, move out with the confidence that God's got your back. Since you know God loves you like that, go out and show someone some love.

~~~~~

Prayer

Compassionate Creator, you are so wonderful and kind, far beyond my capacity to express. Thank you for being you and for providing me with all that I need to navigate the sometimes intimidating maze of life. I trust you with all my heart. I trust what you provide, Amen.

Love Note 83

"Wait on the Lord... (Ps. 27.14a KJV)."

Sometimes the ways of the God can be confusing. We do not always understand what God is doing. And we do not always understand the way God does what God does. One of the things that puzzles us the most is God's timing. Sometimes when we call on God, God moves immediately. We like that type of timing. But there are other times when we call on God and God seems to take God's sweet time. And yet, we can testify that as we look back over our lives at those times when we were confused about what was taking God so long, when God finally showed up, when God finally stepped in, God's timing was perfect! And based on the way things turned out and the lessons we learned, we have to admit that even though God did not do what we wanted, the way we wanted, when we wanted, God's timing was impeccable. In fact, sometimes because of God's timing things not only turned out the way we had hoped, but they turned out even better than what we had hoped! When the Hebrew boys were about to be put in the fiery furnace, God did not come until they were thrown in the fire. God could have intervene earlier to prevent them from even going into the fire. But God's timing was better because God got more glory out of keeping them safe in the midst of the flames than from keeping them from the flames in the first place. God did not show up to keep them from the heat. But God showed up, got in the heat, and kept the heat from them. Today, remind yourself that God is always on time. You may be waiting on God to move and God has not moved yet. Wait on God. Trust in God and you will discover that God is faithful. As you live with that truth today, show someone some love.

~~~~~

Prayer

Faithful God, forgive me for my impatience. Forgive me for the times when I don't trust you enough to wait on you in faith. I know that you have my best interest at heart and I know that you do all things well. So today, I trust you enough to wait. No matter how long, I trust you because you are too kind to be unkind and too wise to make a mistake. If I can trust you with my soul, then I can trust you with my life! So I choose to serve you while I wait on you, because I know that you will come through! Amen

Love Note 84

"Give thanks unto the LORD, for he is good...

(Ps. 107.1 KJV)."

Have you ever stopped long enough to think of just how blessed you really are? It is difficult to think of all God's blessings in your life without your heart being filled with gratitude. It is often the unfortunate yet overwhelming habit of believers to go to God in prayer with the exclusive purpose of seeking personal blessings. To be sure, if there's anyone we ought to go to for blessings, it is God. After all God is the source of our blessings. However, today consider doing something different in your time of prayer and meditation. Do not pray with the primary purpose of asking God for anything. Instead, let your purpose be to thank

God for everything. God has a holy habit of blessing us with such amazing regularity that we have a tendency to take God's blessings for granted. Take time now to thank God for all that God has done, is doing and will do in your life. Realize that, in a real sense, it was God who woke you up this morning, not your alarm clock. God helped you get your job, not just your resume. You work hard on your job to earn money to take care of yourself and your family, but the Bible says that it is God who gives you the power or the strength to get wealth. God has blessed you with health, strength, food, shelter, clothing, friends, family, a job, and most of all, salvation in Christ our Savior. We have a lot to thank God for! Often we go in prayer seeking God's hand so that we can receive something from God, rather than seeking God's face so that we can just spend time with God. Today, seek His face and thank God for all God has done for you, especially for sending you His Son so that we might have life and have it more abundantly. Praise the Lord! Given that God has been so kind to you, go out today and show someone some love.

~~~~~

Prayer

Lord I give you praise and I glorify your name for all that you have done, are doing, and will do in my life! Today, I do not pray to ask for anything. Today, I pray to thank you for everything! Thank you for material and spiritual blessings. Thank you for providing for all of my needs, especially at times when I don't even ask! But most of all, thank you for giving me new life through faith in Jesus Christ! Hallelujah! I praise your name! Amen.

Love Note 85

"In him we have redemption through his blood, the forgiveness of sins, in accordance with the riches of God's grace that he lavished on us with all wisdom and understanding (Eph. 1.7-8)."

To redeem something is to "recover something by payment." It means to "buy back." It can mean, "to obtain a release or restoration of, as from captivity, by paying a ransom." One of the reasons why the gospel is called "good news" is because although our personal sins have disqualified us from a personal relationship with God, God loved us so much that God came in Christ and redeemed us from sin's consequences by means of His own death on the cross. God in Christ died in our place for our sins that we might live. God did for us what we could not do for ourselves. The Scriptures teach that while we were yet sinners, Christ died for us. So, we do not have to remain prisoners of eternal death. We do not have to live in fear of condemnation and the prospect of being eternally separated from our creator because of our shortcomings. The love of God has been expressed by the Son's willingness to pay the price for our sins with His own blood and restore us to perfect communion with the Father. There was nothing we did or could do to earn that. It is a gift, love's gift. So now, as people redeemed by the blood of Christ, we are free to live in love and service to God and others. We do not have to live in fear. We do not have to wonder about our eternal home. By faith we belong to God. And now we are free to do good works that glorify God. This very truth regarding our redemption is a source of endless joy for the believer. We love God only because God first loved us. Hallelujah, we are free! As you walk in that freedom today show someone some love.

~~~~~

Prayer

Savior and redeemer, there are not adequate words to express the joy and gratitude that fills my heart when I think of the exceedingly great love shown for me on Calvary by the death of your Son, Jesus Christ. Thank you Father for restoring me to a relationship with you and for giving me eternal life in your Son. I cherish my new life in You through Jesus. Free from the guilt and shame of my past, and forgiven of all of my sins forever, I am determined to live a life of love, serving others and sharing with others the good news of your grace, mercy and love. In Jesus' name I pray, Amen.

Love Note 86

"Go home and tell the good things that the Lord has done for you (Mk. 5.19)."

One thing that most children seem to have in common is that they love to hear good stories. As a rule, children seem to love hearing bedtime stories read to them. Inevitably, they have a favorite story. No matter how many times you tell it, they never get tired of hearing it. There is a story that believers never tire of hearing or telling. It is a precious story because it is more than simply a story. It is real. The story we believers never grow weary of hearing is that old, old story of Christ and His love. And because Christ has saved our lives and has changed us in ways that only Christ can, we cannot keep that to ourselves. It's hard to keep good news to yourself.

How about you? Has Christ made a difference in your life? Has Jesus changed your whole life? Well if He has, that news is not meant to be kept a secret. It is good news that is meant to be shared. No matter how many times we tell it, because it is so real, and because Christ means so much, we love to tell the story of how good He has been to us. In fact, not only has Christ been good, but Christ keeps on being good to us over and over again. So we always have a story to tell or a testimony to give of the good things that the Lord does for us! So, let's not keep the good news to ourselves. Today tell someone of His love. And since He has shown you love, today show someone some love.

~~~~~

Prayer

God, today I pledge to share the good news of what you have done in my life through Jesus Christ. Thank you for reminding me that the good news of the love of Christ is not simply to be enjoyed, but it is to be

shared with others. As opportunity presents itself, I will share Christ with others. I will indeed tell of the good things that you have done for me. In Jesus name I pray, Amen.

Love Note 87

"Is there anything too hard for God? (Gen. 18.14)."

The words of the chosen devotional are heaven's response to human disbelief. God made a promise to Abraham and Sarah, and the promise was so incredible that Sarah laughed. Have you ever shared something you believed God was going to do in your life and when you shared it people laughed in disbelief? Have you even reflected on some God inspired vision God has given you or some call that God has placed on your life and it seemed so incredible that it was laughable? Well, the truth is that there is nothing too hard for God! It may be out of the reach of human power and may even strain human reason, but it's still not too hard for God. With God, all things are possible. Sarah could not believe that God would bless her with a child, given the fact that she was well past child-bearing age and her husband was old and full of years. But Sarah got the facts mixed up with the Truth. The facts said that she and her husband could never have a child. But the Truth was there is nothing too hard for God! Our limitations are not God's limitations. Our deficiencies are not God's. What hinders us does not hinder God. What a blessed truth! So let the promises of God inspire you and not the confining limits of mere human possibilities. As you move forward, pursuing the plans that God has for your life, when trials, tests, and obstacles stand between you and the promises of God, trust God and move forward in faith. Lizz Wright was correct when she penned the lyrics, "Have you any rivers that seem un-crossable; any mountains you can't tunnel through? God specializes in things that seem impossible and he can do what no other power, Holy Ghost power, can do!" When God makes you a promise, nothing can frustrate the fulfillment of that promise. As you walk today inspired by that truth, show someone some love.

~~~~~

Prayer

Strong and Mighty God, today I rejoice in knowing that indeed, there is nothing too hard for you! So today, by faith, I hand over to you anything and everything in my life that is too difficult for me. Today, I choose to stop being anxious and afraid about how you are going to bring to pass the things that you promised in my life. There are many things that are too hard for me. But there is nothing too hard for you! The possible is my job but the impossible is yours. Lord, have your way. I pray this in the strong name of Jesus Christ, Amen.

Love Note 88

"Neither do I condemn you. Go and leave your life of sin (Jo. 8.11)."

Caught in the very act of adultery by religious leaders, a woman is brought to the Temple courts where Jesus is teaching and forced to stand before the group to be judged by Jesus. The woman was of little consequence to the men who caught her and brought her to the temple gathering. She was a mere pawn in their quest to undermine Jesus. Though she is treated in a dehumanizing way, she is still human. Even though she is treated like a thing by those who caught her, Jesus treats her with a sense of humanity. Once before Jesus, the woman's accusers point out to Jesus that the law says that she should be stoned for her sin. Jesus responds to them by declaring, "Whoever is without sin, cast the first stone." This reminds her accusers who treat her with such cruel, self-righteous insensitivity that they are sinners, too! Her accusers leave, one by one. She is left alone with Jesus. Interestingly enough, Jesus, who the Bible says knew no sin, is the only one qualified to stone her. Yet He refuses. Instead, He shows her kindness and mercy. He declares to her, "Neither do I condemn you." Then He challenges her to "...leave your life of sin." He does not communicate to her that she was not guilty of the sin of adultery, but He does focus on what she could become, rather what she had been guilty of. Contrary to the thinking of some, Jesus did not come to condemn. Jesus came to forgive and set us free to live a life of greater godly possibilities. The Lord desires that we rise above our lives of sin and embrace a delivered life in relationship with him, a life that is rich in mercy and grace, a life of service, sacrifice, peace and joy. Jesus said, 'I come that you have life and it more abundantly." That life is not found living a life separated from Him. That life is found only in a personal relationship with God through Jesus Christ. That relationship is made possible by His sacrifice on the cross of Calvary. There He showed His love for us by giving His life so that we might live! What a wonderful God we serve! If you are living a life of sin, give your life to Christ and learn to walk in the newness of a forgiven life. If you are a believer, reject sin and rise to the life of love and service that God has ordained for you by Christ's love. Live today, knowing that you are not condemned. You are forgiven in Christ and challenged to live your best life! Go, live that life today, by showing someone some love.

~~~~~

Prayer

Oh Lord, you are so merciful and kind. I am forgiven and restored because of you. Your love and forgiveness have set me free. Thank you. Continue to grant me the grace I need to reject a life of sin and live out the life of freedom, love, and service you have called me to live. I am empowered by your challenge to leave my life of sin, because it means that you believe in me. And if you believe in me, then I believe in me too! You have made me brand new. And with your help, today I seek to live like my new self. In Jesus name I pray. Amen.

Love Note 89

"I, John, your brother and companion in the suffering...was on the island of Patmos...On the Lord's Day I was in the Spirit... (Rev. 1.9-10)."

As a fellow sufferer in the faith, John writes to others who are suffering for the sake of Christ. John explains that he has been exiled on the isle of Patmos for preaching the truth about Jesus. Imagine what it would have been like to be isolated on a lonely island, separated by a haunting sea from friends, family and loved ones. It could have been very easy for John, in his despair, to shut his soul off from God, just as his enemies had shut him physically away from his family and friends. But John does not. John lets his misery bring him closer to God and not take him further from God. What do you do with your suffering? Does it make you bitter and resentful toward people and God, or do you draw closer to God knowing that God has sufficient power to sustain you in your situation? When life brings you trials, tests, and suffering, do not let it cause you to turn away from God. Allow it to turn you towards God. Keep your spirit open to His presence, your mind alert to His voice and your heart open to the assurance of His love. Times of sorrow and suffering are when we need God the most. If we keep trusting Him and stay open to God's presence, His healing power and encouraging Spirit can give us the wherewithal we need to handle life's seasons of sorrow, and like John, even in the midst of our trouble, we can be "in the Spirit." Knowing that God is available even in the sorrow and suffering, be available to someone today and show them some love.

~~~~~

Prayer

God I know that life is full of trials and troubles. When those times come, I do not want to be discouraged, faithless, and seduced into turning my back on you. When the tests and trials of life come, teach me to draw closer to you. You are my everything and I need you all of the time, especially when life is difficult. So in times of trouble, show me how to stay convinced of your presence and open to your Spirit. If I do that, I know that you will give me all I need to triumph in the midst of trials and have victory in the face of life's struggles. Thank you Lord for being available to give me what I need to handle anything life brings my way. Praise your Name. In the capable name of Christ I pray, Amen.

Love Note 90

"I, John, your brother and companion in the suffering...was on the island of Patmos...on the Lord's Day I was in the Spirit... (Rev. 1.9-10)."

The enemies of the Apostle John have isolated him on a lonely island called Patmos. I am sure that they put him on the island to stop his influence on others struggling for the faith. But while John is serving his sentence he writes one of his most powerful letters. At one of the loneliest, most trying times of his life, God uses John to give encouragement and hope to others. Some of the most precious literature was written by men who were enduring great trials. Men like D. Bonhoeffer, M. L. King, Ralph Waldo Emerson, and the Apostle Paul. In fact, all of these men did some of their best work while in jail! When we are suffering for the sake of truth, often God gets His best glory and we are the best witnesses we can be, if we would stay available to God. If we do, God can take the sourness of our situation, add the sweetness of His grace and create a drink of joy that will be refreshing to the souls of others. You may not be incarcerated, but you may find yourself in a prison-like situation. Know that even in the midst of that situation God can use you to be a blessing to someone else. So, today, if life seems kind of hard, do not stay home and feel sorry for yourself. Let God use you today to be a blessing to someone else. Go out today and show someone some love.

~~~~~

Prayer

God you are so amazing! You are so sovereign that you can use the negative experiences in my life to serve as a source of blessings to others. So Lord, teach me how to use what happens to me as a learning experience so

that I can encourage someone else who might be going through what I have gone through. Rather than merely feeling sorry for myself, teach me how to use the lessons I learned through my misery to help others who are going through their misery. What the enemy tries to use for evil, you can teach me how to use it for good! In Christ's name I pray, Amen.

Love Note 91

"On the Lord's Day, I was in the Spirit...

(Rev. 1.10)."

John is exiled away from kith and kin. But even though he is separated from people, he is not separated from God. The truth is, there is no place where people or circumstances can put you where you are separated from God. The sea could not separate John from God. Isolation could not separate John from God. His enemies could not separate John from God. John was in exile from people but not from God. That's good news! Nothing can separate us from God. God is forever available to us, no matter what the situation or circumstance. In fact, John was "in the Spirit" on the Lord's Day, right there on that lonely island. John had worship on Patmos! Because God is present wherever we are, then anything is possible wherever we are. Because of the Spirit, John doesn't just serve time, he makes his time serve him! He puts his time to good use and decides that he and God would have unimpeded communion with one another. John was "in the Spirit..." Because he was in the Spirit, he was able to write a book while isolated on the island. The Spirit makes the difference. In the worst place, he was able to do his best work and it was all because of the Spirit! What are you influenced by in times of trouble? What you allow to influence you will determine what you do with your situation. John was influenced by the Spirit and consequently wrote a magnificent message in a miserable situation. Let the Spirit influence you in all situations and then be prepared for incredible things to happen. Today, walk in the Spirit and show someone some love.

~~~~~

Prayer

Lord, today I rejoice knowing that nothing can separate me from you and your love. No matter what happens to me, you are always present and available. So I am not afraid of what will happen today. Just knowing that you are always with me means that I am never alone. But it also means that because you are with me, great things are possible, even in a negative situation! So, I face the day with tip toe anticipation, knowing that if I let your Spirit influence me, no matter what, great things can still happen! Hallelujah! Amen.

Love Note 92

"To those who have been called, who are loved by God the Father and kept by Jesus Christ... (Jude 1b)."

Jude, who identifies himself as "a servant of Jesus Christ and a brother of James," has an insightful way of addressing the community of believers to whom he is writing. At the very beginning of the letter, he refers to the believers in three ways. First he writes that they are "called." Sometimes those of us in the faith only consider preachers to be called. But the truth is every believer is called of God. To be called of God is to be set apart for God. To be called means that you are set aside so that your life can be used by God for God's glory. What an awe-inspiring reality. God has laid claim to our lives by virtue of His Son our Savior, and seeks to use our lives in a way that

God is glorified. Are you cooperating with that call? Can people look at your life and be inspired by how wonderful God is? Jude also refers to his audience as those who are "loved by God the Father." We are loved! How exciting! We are not only saved, but we are cherished by the Father. We are the apple of His eye, special and precious in God's sight. Know that you are deeply loved and cherished by God. And if you want to know just how much God loves you, look at Calvary! You are loved of God and nothing can separate you from God's love. Hallelujah! Finally, Jude says they are "kept by Jesus Christ." We are kept. We are carefully watched over and guarded by the Lord. Like a shepherd watches over his sheep, we are kept, watched over and cared for by the Good Shepherd, Jesus Christ. We are kept - saved by His sacrifice, covered by His blood, forgiven of our sins, protected by His power, preserved by the gift of eternal life. What a wonderful Savior! Yes, we are called, loved and kept. Those are three reasons to give God praise. Because the Lord has been so good to us, let us go out today and show someone some love.

~~~~~

Prayer

Dear God, being in the family of faith sets before me so many spiritual riches that I am moved to give you praise! I have so much to thank you for. But I want to especially thank you for calling me, loving me and keeping me. Thank you for calling someone like me to be used for your glory. That's a miracle. Thank you for loving me so much that you sent you Son for me. I feel special and cherished by you. And thank you for keeping me because I realize that I cannot keep myself. In your marvelous name I pray, Amen.

Love Note 93

"Love the Lord our God with all your heart and all your soul and all your mind and with all your strength (Mark 12.30)."

According to Jesus, this is the most important of all of the commandments. The way the commandment is written, it essentially calls us to love God with everything that we are, to love God mentally, emotionally, spiritually and with all of our strength. It means to love God with all that we are and with all that we have. It means to withhold nothing from God and put nothing or no one before God. It means to love and trust God with our total selves. If there is anyone who is worthy of such total and absolute love, it is our God. Our God created us, sustains us, provides for us, protects us, and loves us deeply, totally and perfectly. God loves us so much that He sent His Son who sacrificed His life that we might have everlasting life! We love God because God first loved us. Inspired by the love, we live in loving relationship with God. To live in a loving relationship with God is to live in trusting obedience to God, convinced that God has our best interest at heart. To live loving God is to live with the blessed assurance that we are loved unconditionally and that God's perfect love was demonstrated by Christ at Calvary's hill. What a wonderful God we serve. To live in the love of God is to experience wholeness, joy, peace, purpose and fulfillment. It is as we live, loving God and enjoying God's love for us through Jesus the Christ that we begin to experience life at its highest and best. Love God today and let God's love for you flow through you to someone else.

~~~~~

Prayer

God today I give myself to you afresh. Today I dare to declare again that I am yours...all of me. Everything I am, everything I have and everything I hope to be, I surrender to you today. With all that I have and all that I am I love you. And Lord I realize that love is not mere words. So with the help of your grace, I will demonstrate my love today by seeking to live led by your Spirit, inspired by your command to love, and in obedience to your Word. Please Lord, use me today and be glorified in my life. In the matchless name of Jesus I pray, Amen.

Love Note 94

"Love your neighbor as yourself (Mk. 12.31)."

Fast on the heels of Jesus teaching that we are to love God with our total selves is His teaching that we are commanded to love our neighbor as ourselves. One cannot claim to love God and not love one's neighbor. The two are inextricably bound together. The Bible says elsewhere that we cannot claim to love a God whom we cannot see and hate our neighbor whom we can see! The command to love God is a call to love all those whom God has created. We are commanded to love our neighbor. Our neighbor is anyone, especially anyone in need. Jesus declares that our love for others ought to be like the love we have for ourselves. This presupposes that we have a healthy love for ourselves. When we have a healthy self-love, we take care of ourselves, respect ourselves and seek the best for ourselves. We are called to have that kind and quality of love for others. It is not a love primarily rooted in how we feel. It is agape love which seeks the best for another, regardless of how they behave toward us. It is not, therefore, primarily a feeling, but an act of the will. This love is a verb, not a noun. It is a decision to do right by another, regardless of how he behave towards you. To love with this kind of love means we need the aid and assistance of God. We need divine help. We need the Spirit of Christ! When we give our lives to Him, we can live, allowing His Spirit to live and love through us. We cannot love like that on our own. However, "we can do all things through Christ who strengthens us." So today, go out and show someone that love!

~~~~~

Prayer

Loving Father, thank you for your love. Now, by your Spirit, teach me how to love everyone. Everyone bears in them your divine image, so all are valuable to you and are worthy of your love. Help me to show love, especially to the downtrodden, outcast, and oppressed, because I know you have a special place in your heart for the most vulnerable, "the least of these." Deliver me from selfishness and make me sensitive to the needs of others. I pray that all believers who follow you will commit to a life of love toward our neighbors until the world realizes that you are love and that the greatest antidote for the problems of humanity is the power of divine love. In the name of He who is love incarnate I pray, Amen.

Love Note 95

"Faith without works is dead (Jas. 2.26 KJV)."

James makes the powerful and insightful declaration that faith without works is like a body without breath. That faith is dead. A body without breath is a body with no signs that it has any life at all. So it is useless. A faith that has no works is a faith that is showing no signs that it is alive at all. It, too, is useless. The authenticity of a person's faith is revealed in the deeds that the person does. Jesus says that you can tell a tree by the fruit it bears. If it is an apple tree, then sooner or later you will see evidence of its identity by the presence of apples on the limbs. If a person has had an authentic encounter with Christ by faith and is changed, then there ought to be evidence of that change. That evidence would be the behavior of that believer. If a person has the Spirit of Christ, then that person will show the fruit of it by acting like Christ. Being a Christian is not simply subscribing to a set of beliefs. It is receiving Christ by faith and being absolutely committed to living in obedience to Christ. We are no longer at the center. Christ is. Christ is not only our Savior, but He is our Lord. Christ said, "Why do you call me Lord, Lord and do not do what I say?" So, the way people know that we have been saved by Christ and are committed to Christ, is that we live in obedience to the Spirit and teachings of Christ. The old folks in the church where I grew up said it like this, "If you've got good religion you ought to show some sign." The sign of authentic conversion by Christ is a commitment to Christ and behaving like Christ. We are not saved by good works, but we are saved to do good works. That's not faith plus works. That's faith that works! If you are really saved by grace through faith, go out and prove it by showing someone some love.

~~~~~

Prayer

Gracious God, when you saved me, you changed me and called me out of a life of sin and selfishness into a life of loving service and sacrifice. Let my life reflect a faith that serves others so that you are glorified in the world. That's my desire today. I want to show just how real my faith is by the life I live and the way I serve. Give me grace for that today. In Jesus' name I pray, Amen.

Love Note 96

"But Lot's wife looked back, and she became a pillar of salt (Gen. 19.26)."

We are not made to run forward and look backwards at the same time. Any professional runner will tell you that when you are running as fast as you can in an effort to reach a particular goal, you have to stay focused on the path ahead of you. Lot's wife, along with her husband and family, were instructed by an angel to run to safety. The city they were once residents of was about to be destroyed and time was of the essence. They were told to leave immediately and run to higher ground and not to look back. However, Lot's wife yielded to the temptation to look back, and as soon as she did, she turned into a pillar of salt. Isn't that what happens whenever we try to live forward and backwards at the same time? If we are going to make progress in our lives, we need to learn to let what's behind us go. Some have suggested that Lot's wife's looking back ended in her being turned into a pillar of salt because it was a look longing for what was behind her. Her direction did not match her desires. She had a divided heart. She was running forward, but she was looking and longing for what was behind her. She was not really committed to going forward, and her progress was paralyzed. She was turned into a pillar of salt, a statute, a life at a standstill. Until we learn to leave some things in the past and focus on moving forward in a hurry, then we will end up paralyzing our on progress and finding our lives at a standstill. If you want to escape the debilitating mistakes, pains and negative experiences of the past and move into the healing, empowering and liberating possibilities of the future, then you will have to learn that you cannot live in the past and in the future at the same time. Don't look back. Move forward and claim the destiny that God has ordained for you. Do not waste precious energy on the regrets of the past. Reserve your precious energies for God's vision of your future and run forward with everything you've got. As you run today, remember, someone might be struggling with his past, so show someone some love.

~~~~~

Prayer

God, I know that I am created to move forward. You saved me so that I can grow, make progress, and move forward on my personal pilgrimage to spiritual maturity. Grant me continued courage and strength to never get stuck looking behind me. Teach me to daily release the things that hold me back and keep me from moving toward my destiny. Whether they are people or powers, I want nothing to keep me from the future you have bequeathed to me. I am free to become all that you desire for me, so I won't look back! In Jesus mighty Name I pray, Amen.

Love Note 97

"In the name of Jesus Christ of Nazareth walk. Taking him by the right hand, he helped him up, and instantly the man's feet and ankles became strong (Ac. 3.6b-7)."

This devotional is recorded to show God's finest apostles ministering to a lame man begging outside of the temple gate. It is a powerful and touching scene. Begging for money, the lame man looks to Peter and John for financial assistance. To his surprise, he does not get what he desires. This is simply because God always reserves the right to give us better than what we expect. The lame man asked these men of God for money, but they declared that they had none. Money has its place, but there are some things that money cannot buy.

Instead of giving the lame man money, these men ministered to him in such a way that was greater than his wildest dreams. They declared, "In the name of Jesus Christ of Nazareth..." This declaration was designed to let this lame man know that the power that was about to give him the capacity to walk, was not from these men. This miracle would happen because of the power of God. What is so touching about the miracle is that once Peter declares that he walk, he and John do not step back and watch the lame man struggle to his feet on his own. Instead, the Bible says that Peter reached down and took the man by his hand and helped him to his feet. Notice that in order for Peter to do this, he had to look down and reach down. This fact reminds us that the only time we should ever look down on anyone is when we are reaching down to help him up. As Peter pulled him up, the lame man felt the power of God through his limbs and he jumped to his feet and began to walk. A miracle took place and a man who could not walk was able to walk, all because of heaven's power and the helping hands of two compassionate people of God. Let them be your inspiration. Pledge today to let God use you to somehow help put someone on their feet, whether it be emotionally, spiritually or financially. Today, be an instrument of God to empower someone's life. Today, go out, reach down, and show someone some love.

~~~~~

Prayer

Dear Lord, there are many people in our community who are down and feel too helpless to get up. I pray that you would give me the faith, power and love to reach down to those in need and help pull them to their feet in the name of Jesus. I know that is what you want because when I was down and helpless, crippled by my sins, and you didn't just reach down, you came down in the person of your Son our Savior Jesus Christ and lifted me by your love! I pray for all believers everywhere that we become your hands of help and healing for those who are down and forgotten. Today Lord, use me to lift someone who's down. In Jesus lifting, loving Name I pray, Amen.

Love Note 98

"He jumped to his feet and began to walk. Then he went with them into the temple courts, walking and jumping and praising God (Ac. 3.8)."

Yesterday we saw how a lame man who was begging for money at the temple gate was made the recipient of a miracle. Two men of God, by the power of God, and in the name of Jesus, helped this man do what he could not do all of his life - walk! Imagine what must have gone on in the mind of this man. Imagine the extraordinary joy that must have flooded his heart as he stood up on strong legs that had never been able to hold him up before. He was now strong in a place where he had always been weak. He was now realizing the potential that he had never thought possible. He was now

286

experiencing victory in a place where he had only
known defeat. This is what happens when the Lord
takes control of your life. He gives you freedom by
giving you power to do what you could not do
before. He gives you power over what used to have
power over you. This man's reaction to the love and
power of God in his life makes perfect sense. He
went into the temple walking, leaping, and praising
God. There are times when extravagant praise is in
order. Without shame, hesitation, or reservation,
this former lame man used the very legs that had
been lame to praise God. Since God has blessed our
lives in so many miraculous ways, we ought to use
our lives like this man used his legs - to give glory to
God! It was the power of God and the assistance of
two disciples that made this man's lame legs leap up
and dance. Show someone some love today and
maybe they too will find a reason to dance!

~~~~~

Prayer

Father, you have done a miracle in my life. You have made me whole. Forgive me for taking your goodness for granted and then withholding the praise. Forgive me for those times when I have been so preoccupied with what people would think of me that I was quiet about your goodness in my life. Since you were not ashamed to save me, then I will never be ashamed to praise you! Your goodness has brought me joy! Today, I will share that joy with others, telling them of your goodness. In Jesus name I pray, Amen.

Love Note 99

"When all the people saw him walking and praising God they recognized him as the same man who used to sit at the temple gate called beautiful... (Ac. 3.9-10a KJV)."

The changed life of the lame man in the text may have been personal, but it was not private. Once he was healed, he became joyously demonstrative, publicly praising God and trying out those newly healed legs. People noticed that he had been changed. They noticed that he was not in the same place as they were used to seeing him. He used to sit at the gate, but now he is in the Temple. His new condition changed his location. God has a way of changing your life so that you no longer have the desire to frequent the places you used to frequent.

A new you often means new places. The people noticed that the lame man was not doing what he used to do. He used to beg, but he begged because he was lame. He did what he did because there was an area of weakness in his life. It is amazing what we will resort to because we are just too weak to do anything else. However, his strengthened legs gave him a new lease on life. New legs meant a new destiny. Because the power of God had given this man new strength, he could leave behind what he used to do. Being liberated by the power of God meant that this man did not have to resign himself to his weakness, but he could pursue a new life with new practices and possibilities. New power means a new future. What God did for the lame man, he can do for us. When we surrender to God's life, love and salvation, we are given power to leave behind the life and behaviors our weaknesses had sentenced us to. We did what we did before because, in a real sense, we were too weak to do anything else. However, once we surrender to the power of Christ, new power gives us new potential, new behavior and new destiny. If God's love has empowered you to begin to live a brand new life, then today, in gratitude, go out and show someone some love.

~~~~~

Prayer

Lord, I praise you for all you have done for me. I stand in awe of how you have lifted and empowered my life in ways I had never dreamed possible. Because of your deliverance and power, I can do what I couldn't do before. Thank you Lord! Today, because of the power of your Spirit in my life, I have new hope, a new future, and a new destiny! I have left behind where I used to go because I'm not the same. Hallelujah!

Where I still struggle, I need your strength. Where still sin, I need your forgiveness. Still, I know I'm new and I will never be the same again. Thank you for a new life, with new possibilities and a brand new future. Thank you for my new legs! In Jesus Name I pray, Amen.

Love Note 100

"...and they were filled with wonder and amazement at what had happened to him (Ac. 3.10b KJV)."

Has it ever occurred to you that the miraculous things that God is doing in your life are not just for you? It is true that God has a way of doing extraordinary and miraculous things in our lives that are designed to bring us unspeakable joy. However, while what God does may bring personal joy, it may also be meant to bring about public awareness of God's goodness and love. That's what happened to the lame man who used to sit by the gate but was miraculously healed by the power of God. His life was changed forever. His changed life was meant to be a witness to others of God's amazing love and power. The miracle happened to him, but it was also meant to be seen by the people who knew him. They saw the change and were filled with wonder and amazement. It is clear that God did not mean for this miracle to happen in a corner, but in full view of the public's eyes. God used the wonder of this man's miraculous change to stir the hearts of those who stood nearby so that they might be open to the message of the gospel of Jesus Christ. In fact, it was because people were astonished at what God had done in the life of this man, that Peter had a chance to preach, and many people believed (Ac. 4.4.). Do not keep the great things that God is doing in your life a secret. Go public with the change that Jesus is making in your life. You may not be able to preach or teach, but you can let the great things that God is doing in your life be a testimony of the love and power of Jesus Christ. When others witness the change that Jesus is making in you, then perhaps they, too, might be persuaded to believe. As evidence of the change that Jesus is making in your life, go out today and show someone some love.

~~~~~

Prayer

Gracious God, I praise and glorify you because you are worthy to be praised. I am thankful that you have chosen to bless me. But I am exceptionally grateful that you have chosen to bless me so that my life can be a blessing to someone else! I know you have done and are doing a great work in me because you want to put my change on public display. You desire that I be a walking billboard, advertising to others how good a God you are. So today, use me Lord to advertise your goodness. Use the contrast between my past and my present to glorify your own name. Use my life as a witness of Christ's goodness, power and love. Let my conduct and conversation be evidence of your goodness and grace today until people are in awe of you and even desire to know you for themselves. Do it Lord. In Jesus matchless name I pray, Amen.

~~~~~~~~~~~~~~~ *Notes* ~~~~~~~~~~~~~~~

_____

_____

_____

_____

_____

_____

_____

_____

_____

_____

_____

_____

_____

_____

_____

_____

_____

_____

~~~~~~~~~~~~~~ *Notes* ~~~~~~~~~~~~~~

_____

_____

_____

_____

_____

_____

_____

_____

_____

_____

_____

_____

_____

_____

_____

_____

_____

_____

_____

~~~~~~~~~~~~~~ *Notes* ~~~~~~~~~~~~~~

~~~~~~~~~~~~~~ *Notes* ~~~~~~~~~~~~~~

~~~~~~~~~~~~~~~ *Notes* ~~~~~~~~~~~~~~~

~~~~~~~~~~~~~~~ *Notes* ~~~~~~~~~~~~~~~

~~~~~~~~~~~~~~~ *Notes* ~~~~~~~~~~~~~~~

~~~~~~~~~~~~~~ *Notes* ~~~~~~~~~~~~~~

~~~~~~~~~~~~~~~ *Notes* ~~~~~~~~~~~~~~~

~~~~~~~~~~~~~~ *Notes* ~~~~~~~~~~~~~~

~~~~~~~~~~~~~~~ *Notes* ~~~~~~~~~~~~~~~

~~~~~~~~~~~~~~~ *Notes* ~~~~~~~~~~~~~~~

Author Bio:

Dr. F. Bruce Williams is the Senior Pastor at Bates Memorial Baptist Church in Louisville, Kentucky. He is frequently asked to serve as an instructor and guest preacher for various community wide events, lectures, seminars, workshops, and revivals throughout the country. Dr. Williams is married to Dr. L. Michelle Williams and they are the proud parents of two adult daughters. More information about Dr. Williams can be found on his website at www.fbrucewilliamsministries.com.

Other Books by Dr. Williams

Gideon- A Hero In the Making

You Can Have As Far As You Can See

Made in the USA
Charleston, SC
23 October 2015